* * * * *

"This is a wonderful bridge between the past, present, and future for m-spec people. It offers clarity, guidance, and a floor upon which to land. A challenging, seasoned read filled with hope that has known despair, and vigor that has known various states of being."

– J.R. Yussuf, author of *Dear Bi Men: A Black Man's Perspective on Power, Consent, Breaking Down Binaries, and Combating Erasure*

* * * * *

"*It Ain't Over Til The Bisexual Speaks* is a beautiful brilliant bi+ book. It does a wonderful job of honouring its bi+ activist/anthology predecessors as well as pointing towards vital directions for bi+ futures. The collection is curated with deep care and attention to detail, situating bi+ movements appropriately in relation to capitalist/colonialist histories, immutable understandings of gender/sexuality, and current forms of bodymind normativity and related culture wars and global politics. It was moving indeed to feel the commitment and compassion of the bi+ activists included in this collection, and to be reminded of just what they're up against when fighting for the freedom of all who are impacted by bi+, and intersecting, oppressions."

– Meg-John Barker, co-author of *Life Isn't Binary* and *Queer: A Graphic History*

* * * * *

* * * * *

"A beautiful collection of voices which truly represents the great diversity of our bi+/mspec community. With a broad range of experiences from all corners of the bisexual spectrum, this book breaks down the many assumptions and stereotypes that persist against bisexual people in our society today. A fascinating read for anybody, whether you're familiar with the bi community or new to the topic. The kind of book I wish I'd had when I was growing up!"

– Mark Cusack, Bisexual author, educator and coach

* * * * *

"I found this collection wide ranging in perspective, thought-provoking, well-written, and much-needed. Particularly impressive is the focus on the intersection of bisexual identity with other identities: disability, neurodivergence, nationality, immigration status, race, gender, and more. If you read this collection, you will learn something new. My advice to anyone reading this: please go out and get yourself a copy!"

– Robyn Ochs, educator, speaker, grassroots activist, and editor of *Bi Women Quarterly* and two anthologies: the 42-country collection *Getting Bi: Voices of Bisexuals Around the World* and *RECOGNIZE: The Voices of Bisexual Men*

* * * * *

IT AIN'T OVER TIL
THE BISEXUAL SPEAKS

of related interest

Bisexual Men Exist
A Handbook for Bisexual,
Pansexual and M-Spec Men
Vaneet Mehta
ISBN: 978 1 78775 7 196
eISBN: 978 1 78775 7 196

Bi the Way
The Bisexual Guide to Life
ISBN: 978 1 78775 2 900
eISBN: 978 1 78775 2 917

Non-Binary Lives
An Anthology of Intersecting Identities
*Edited by Jos Twist, Ben Vincent,
Meg-John Barker and Kat Gupta*
ISBN: 978 1 78775 3 396
eISBN: 978 1 78775 3 402

It Ain't Over Til the Bisexual Speaks

An Anthology of Bisexual Voices

Edited by Vaneet Mehta
& Lois Shearing

Jessica Kingsley Publishers
London and Philadelphia

First published in Great Britain in 2024 by Jessica Kingsley Publishers
An imprint of Hodder & Stoughton Ltd
An Hachette Company

1

This book contains mentions of biphobia, transphobia and sexual assault.

A CIP catalogue record for this title is available from the British Library
and the Library of Congress

ISBN 978 1 83997 1 952
eISBN 978 1 83997 1 969

Printed and bound in Great Britain by TJ Books Limited

Jessica Kingsley Publishers' policy is to use papers that are natural,
renewable and recyclable products and made from wood grown in
sustainable forests. The logging and manufacturing processes are expected
to conform to the environmental regulations of the country of origin.

Jessica Kingsley Publishers
Carmelite House
50 Victoria Embankment
London EC4Y 0DZ

www.jkp.com

To Lani Kaʻahumanu, thank you for the title inspiration.

To all of our writers, thank you for your dedication, hard work and passion; not just with this book but to bisexual activism in general.

– Lumpi and Vaneet

For Vaneet, for being not only the one person I could survive a project like this with, but with whom a friendship has blossomed throughout that I will cherish always.

– Lumpi

For Lumpi, for being an endless source of knowledge and inspiration for me. You taught me everything I know about the history of bisexual activism and I am forever grateful to call you a friend.

– Vaneet

Contents

Welcome

Anthologies have always been a staple of bisexual literature. From *Bisexual Politics: Theories, Queries, and Visions*, published in 1995 (Tucker, 1995) to *The Bi-ble* Volumes 1 and 2, published in 2017 and 2019 respectively (Nickodemus & Desmond, 2017/2019), anthologies have been the backbone of the bisexual movement through the decades, giving us the space to talk about the rich and varied activism taking place in our community.

The reasons why anthologies have, and continue to be, so central to our movement are twofold. First, until recently, there was a complete lack of support from mainstream publishers in publishing bisexual non-fiction books. In some cases, there was hesitancy to publish such books. In others, it had never occurred to these publishers that they should or that there even were bisexual thinkers, writers and theorists that they *could* publish. This is both a result – and function – of bi-erasure.

A consequence of this is that many bisexual authors, activists and theorists pooled their resources and turned to independent publishers to produce collective works which explored the underrepresented and often hidden lived experiences of bi people. Some examples of this include *Rec.og.nize: The Voices of Bisexual Men*, published by Bisexual Resource Center (Ochs & Williams, 2015), *Purple Prose*, published by Thorntree Press (Harrad, 2016) and the aforementioned *The Bi-ble* duology, published by Monstrous Regiment.

The second reason bi anthologies were so popular, as we have already alluded to, is plurality. Plurality lives at the heart of both anthology as a genre and the bisexual movement – indeed, plurality lives at the heart of bisexuality itself. The bisexual community is vastly diverse. Statistics from the UK (Government Equalities Office, 2018) show that trans people are more likely to identify as bisexual than gay, lesbian or straight. Statistics from the US show that bisexual people are more likely to be disabled (Movement Advancement Project, 2019) and more likely to live below the poverty level (Badgett, Choi & Wilson, 2019) than gay, lesbian or straight people. Our sexuality doesn't exist in a vacuum; we all hold a multitude of different identities and, for bisexual people, we so often belong to multiple marginalized groups.

Not only are we a varied group in the plurality of our identities, but even our bisexuality itself comes in many different forms. Bisexuality allows for so many ways to desire and to express that desire. No two people who use the word bisexual will experience attraction to multiple genders in the same way (they may not even be attracted to the same genders as each other) and the way that desire is felt and expressed will be influenced by their own gender, as well as race, class, body, language, culture and identity. Celebrating that plurality has always been central to the bisexual movement – as the popular saying "embrace the power of *and*" suggests. And it is this essence that we have tried to capture with this anthology. We have writers from numerous different backgrounds with a range of different experiences, no two of which are alike. Our writers explore a multitude of different areas, from navigating survivorship to making a safe space within your own home. They explore how bisexuality intersects with other identities, including race, class and disability, touching on both the frictions within the bi+ movement itself as well as the experiences of living within these liminal spaces.

While there are topics that we wanted but, for a number of reasons, weren't able to cover in this anthology, we have tried our utmost to ensure that we have covered a breadth of viewpoints and experiences that make our community and highlight how we must work together to support every marginalized person. Can we truly say bi people are free if bi people of colour are still experiencing racism in bi/queer spaces? Can we truly say bi people are free if our safe spaces aren't accessible to bi disabled people? Can we truly say bi people are free if our events price out poor bi people? Ultimately, none of us are free until all of us are free.

The anthology this one most draws inspiration from is the previously mentioned *Bisexual Politics: Theories, Queries, and Visions*, edited by Naomi S. Tucker (1995). The book is a snapshot of the politics, discourse and organizing bubbling in the bisexual movement. It captured the views of bi writers and theorists on several of the most pressing issues of the time. For example, in "Essay for the Inclusion of Transsexuals", Kory Martin-Damon argues for the inclusion of trans people – which was a radical stance at the time – in what was then known as the lesbian, gay, and bisexual movement, saying, "The inclusion of transgendered people can only empower any movement (such as the bisexual movement) that seeks to bring about changes in social mores and gender norms" (p.249). While many other anthologies exploring bisexual lives have appeared since, none has contributed to the politically charged conversations started by *Bisexual Politics: Theories, Queries, and Visions*. That is what *It Ain't Over Til the Bisexual Speaks* sets out to do – to capture the conversations, politics and organizing of the bisexual movement in the 2020s.

We also took inspiration from Lani Ka'ahumanu's speech "It Ain't Over 'Til the Bisexual Speaks". In 1993, Ka'ahumanu was told she could only speak for two minutes as the final speaker at that year's March on Washington. This came after facing mounting biphobia from within the gay and lesbian movement, despite having been a dedicated activist for decades. In the speech, she says:

> Are bisexuals visible yet?
> Are bisexuals organized yet?
> Are bisexuals accountable yet?
> You bet your sweet ass we are!
> Bisexuals are here,
> and we're queer.
> Bisexual pride
> speaks to the truth
> of behavior and identity.

Three decades later, there is still a strong belief that the bisexual community has nothing to say that could be of interest or use to the wider queer community. In this text, we hope to show that the bi movement is still as active and political as ever, even in the face of erasure and a complete lack of monetary support from lesbian, gay, bisexual, transgender, queer/questioning, intersex and other (LGBTQIA+) organizations. But, we want to be clear: just because we have spoken, it sure ain't over. This anthology draws on a rich history within the bisexual movement, building on the many bisexual anthologies that came before it. We hope this book will be seen as a worthy contribution to this history and will serve to inspire and galvanize a new wave of bi activism, organizing, collaborating, agitating, community building, coming out, coming together, and finding joy in our shared struggle.

References

Badgett, M.L., Choi, S.K. & Wilson, B.D.M. (2019). *LGBT Poverty in the United States: A study of differences between sexual orientation and gender identity groups*. Los Angeles, CA: The Williams Institute.

Government Equalities Office. (2018). *National LGBT Survey: Research Report*. www.gov.uk/government/publications/national-lgbt-survey-summary-report.

Harrad, K. (2016). *Purple Prose: Bisexuality in Britain*. Portland, OR: Thorntree Press.

Ka'ahumanu, L. (1995). "It Ain't Over 'Til the Bisexual Speaks." In: N. Tucker, L. Highleyman, and R. Kaplan (eds), *Bisexual Politics, Theories, Queries, and Visions*. New York: The Haworth Press, 63-68.

Movement Advancement Project. (2019). *LGBT People with Disabilities*. www.lgbtmap.org/lgbt-people-disabilities.

Nickodemus, L. & Desmond, E. (2017/2019). *The Bi-ble*. Volumes 1 and 2. Edinburgh: Monstrous Regiment.

Ochs, R. & Williams, H.S. (2015). *Rec.og.nize: The Voices of Bisexual Men*. Boston, MA: Bisexual Resource Center.

Tucker, N.S. (ed.) (1995). *Bisexual Politics: Theories, Queries, and Visions*. London, New York, NY: Harrington Park.

CHAPTER 1

Bisexuality Is Freedom

Finding Our History

Mel Reeve

Mel Reeve (she/her) is a writer and lapsed archivist living in Glasgow. As an archivist, she has worked on a wide variety of projects, with organizations such as the National Library of Scotland, Glasgow Women's Library and more. She runs the Bi History project (@BiHistory), which aims to celebrate, promote and preserve the history of the bisexual+ community. As a writer, her fiction and narrative non-fiction work has been published widely, including by 404 Ink, Monstrous Regiment Publishing, Knight Errant Press, The Skinny, Autostraddle, and more. In 2020, she won the Glasgow Women's Library Bold Types short story prize and was nominated as one of YWCA Scotland's "30 Under 30". She co-runs the FOMA Press zine distro (@fomapress), and has created several popular zines, including a sold-out exploration of queer medieval history through fact and fiction. Her work often explores themes of identity, queer history and the natural world. She can be found on social media @melreeve and at home with her beloved cat.

For many of us, looking to our history is the starting point for how we understand ourselves. It gives us context; a shape and dimension to apply to our own complicated experience of existing. We can look to the paths of those who have come before to see where we might go next. It can also give community, a feeling of belonging and comfort – in sharp contrast to the alienation and loneliness that many people, especially those from marginalized communities, encounter in their daily life. What happens then, when we are denied access to our histories? What happens if we do not even know we have a community to look back on and be part of? For marginalized people, the experience of finding ourselves in the past can be even more vital, and yet so often these are the histories that are ignored, forgotten, dismissed or erased.

The phrase "bisexual history" feels comfortable to me now but there was a time when it felt alien and complicated, like a question I was trying to ask without permission, or an intrusion on something that was not mine. The words did not seem to fit neatly together; in fact, they felt somehow in conflict with each other. Coincidentally, as I was developing my understanding of myself, I was also beginning a career working in heritage as an archivist.

As part of the heritage community, archivists are responsible for collecting, managing and preserving the records that people (particularly historians and researchers) use as sources to understand and describe the past. This can be exciting; perhaps being donated a marvellous collection of letters from someone's attic that perfectly describe the life of a long-dead relative, and in so doing reveal what it was like to live at that moment in history. It can also be highly repetitive work that requires a great deal of focus, meticulously cataloguing all those letters to ensure that if someone wants to find a letter relating to a specific topic, they will be able to do so. Those letters are records of a time and a place, and of the people who lived then;

these records (whatever form they may come in) are the materials that constitute an archive: records of people, places, things, lives and societies.

It made sense, then, that as I developed my understanding of how we record and manage records of our histories, I also found in myself a hunger to find records of bisexual+ people and communities, within existing archive collections. Archives are often held by large institutions, and all too often the histories they contain are representative of the power structures of our world, prioritizing the voices of privileged, white, heterosexual men. Marginalized communities have historically operated outside the mainstream, whether because of criminalization, prejudice or their own rejection of traditional structures. It is hardly surprising that these marginalized voices are often harder to find represented in traditional record forms. The nature of archiving and the structures that support it sadly often exacerbate this divide rather than working actively to challenge it. Records of LGBTQ+ and other marginalized communities are often lost or ignored because of the ephemeral nature of a community trying to protect itself from the prejudice of wider society, and the inherently exclusionary nature of many traditional archive practices.

Early in my own searching for bisexual+ history, I was repeatedly challenged by resources that declared they contained records of LGBTQ+ history, but showed only explicit evidence of lesbian and gay people and their communities. I knew on some level that this did not exclude the existence of bisexual+ people entirely. I myself had lived the experience of being in a queer space and being presumed not to be a part of that community, and then in the rest of the world being presumed straight. I knew not being able to find these records didn't mean there weren't any bisexual+ people in those spaces, but I wanted desperately to see physical evidence of my community naming itself as such. I wanted to know if other people had been proud to be bisexual, because that felt like permission for me to find pride in who I am. What I found in the end changed how I saw myself and the work I did in heritage, and led me to create the Bi History project (@BiHistory on Instagram and X (formerly known as Twitter)).

At the beginning of the project I was sharing on social media what felt like rare and precious glimpses into a world I had only dared to hope had existed. In finding records of the bisexual+ community and its rich, wonderful, complicated history, I found permission to be my own authentic self and to explore and understand my own identity. I also began to question how we place value on archival records, and how we excuse the lack of representation found in many archive collections – something I was feeling increasingly aware of and uncomfortable with. I've seen repeated evidence throughout my career in heritage that many people do not even realize that bisexual+ people exist within LGBTQ+ records unless they are named as such, and even then that this valuable history can still be erased or ignored. This is a disservice to the historical LGBTQ+ communities and individuals themselves, and also offers a reductive, minimizing view of the true reality of the richness of LGBTQ+ history and what that can offer us looking back.

As I began to realize how much of the bisexual+ history I knew existed was missing or underrepresented, even from explicitly queer archive collections, the Bi History project developed into something else. It became somewhere for me to express my frustration that bisexual+ history was seen as separate from LGBTQ+ history, or was just straight-up ignored. The project then became a tool for me to advocate for the inclusion of bisexual+ people in archival collections, and in our discussions of LGBTQ+ history.

The Bishopsgate Institute in London now holds the Bi History archive collection which I gathered over the course of workshops and events, and through interaction with other bisexual+ groups. I also consulted and offered guidance to heritage institutions and groups looking to be more inclusive. I have spoken with many different people from across the world through the work of the Bi History project. Repeatedly they tell me how meaningful seeing evidence of our community's history is. It can be life-changing for people to see evidence of those that have lived before who were, in some ways, a little like them – particularly when we are more accustomed to hearing about who we are and how we must be from people outside the community.

So much of contemporary discussion around bisexual+ identity still revolves around what bisexual+ people are permitted to do, say and be. Biphobia exists strongly in many LGBTQ+ spaces, as well as in the wider world. Much biphobia is wrapped up in the idea that bisexual+ people do not have a right to their space within the queer community, that we only have a partial claim to queerness, and therefore any space we do take up is somehow inherently problematic or requires caveats. I had myself internalized much of this rhetoric. The damage this can cause is something I understand well on a personal level, but I think it's more important to consider what it can do structurally and to those most at risk because of the intersecting combination of other structural prejudices such as racism.

At its worst, biphobia puts the lives of bisexual+ refugees at risk when seeking asylum; there are several recorded cases of bisexual+ asylum seekers having their applications for asylum rejected or questioned because they are not believed to be bisexual, despite the genuine risk to their safety (Delaram, 2019). This is perhaps the most extreme consequence of biphobia, but it shows the importance of including and respecting bisexual+ people within LGBTQ+ communities.

If we are to advocate for the safety and respect of all bisexual+ people, for me that should begin with the fundamental understanding that bisexual+ people have always been a major part of the LGBTQ+ community's history. This is one way to reinforce the fact that bisexual+ people have a right to space within the wider community, we have unique experiences as part of the LGBTQ+ community, and we are in need of support and recognition by the wider community.

We've considered why bisexual+ history is important, so it makes sense to actually look at some of that history. One of the first recorded uses of the word "bisexual" in the English language in a context that relates to how we use it today was in 1892, in a book by American neurologist Charles Gilbert Chaddock. Before this point, we mainly see evidence of it being used to refer to intersex people, and as a biological term in reference to plant reproduction: "–bi", as in two, "sexual", as in having two sexes. Chaddock was perhaps the first time the term was used in a published work in reference to someone who engaged in sexual activity with (as he defined it) male and female partners. From this starting point, the word has developed over time and is now used to mean someone who is attracted to people of all genders. Pansexuality, sexual fluidity and queer are other identifiers that can be used by people experiencing attraction to people of the same and different genders. The term pansexual has existed and been in use since at least the late 1960s (Steinmetz, 2020), while describing the idea that sexuality could change and develop as being "sexuality fluid" is generally credited to the work of psychologist Lisa M. Diamond in the 2000s (Diamond, 2008).

To look at a specific example of bisexual+ history, if you google "famous early bisexuals" or something similar, your search results will likely include Edna St Vincent Millay (1892–1950). Edna had relationships with men and women throughout her life, even after her marriage, and is described by Wikipedia as one of the first openly bisexual people in America, although it does not seem she ever used that word herself.

The relatively easy availability of records about her life is directly linked to her place in society as a white, upper-class person, which must remind us whose voices are less readily available and why.

When exploring any LGBTQ+ history we need to think carefully about how we use language, and what implications that can have. Our modern understanding of LGBTQ+ identity applies terms to identities, experiences and concepts that have existed across all cultures for all of history. These terms are generally Western and relatively new, so there is some difficulty in applying them to someone who cannot advocate for themselves in how they would like to be defined, and did not have access to the vocabulary we now use.

That said, I think there's a huge amount of value in exploring and celebrating LGBTQ+ history and ensuring that it is recognized and acknowledged. If cis, heterosexual people can look into the past and see representation of themselves, we should be able to as well. Particularly with bisexual+ history, there is a strong perception that it's somehow revisionist to apply the bisexual label retroactively. While there seems to be a slightly higher level of comfort for LGBTQ+ people to describe figures from history as "lesbian" or "gay", the same cannot be said of bisexuality. I would suggest that this is in part because of the biphobic implication that describing someone as bisexual lessens their queerness; if we refer to a historical figure as bisexual, for some that feels like an insult rather than a celebration of our shared community's heritage. This may also be due to so-called marriages of convenience which occurred throughout history, where queer people entered into a marriage with a member of a different gender, as was expected of them, regardless of their own sexuality. For example, when looking for LGBTQ+ history we may come across records of people who had documented relationships with women, and also married men. Many of these people may well have only experienced same-gender attraction but were forced to marry to survive, either directly or through societal pressures. All of these people still form part of the history of the LGBTQ+ community, and the experience of trying to conform before you understand your own sexuality fully, or because of the environment you are living in, is one that many LGBTQ+ people across the world can still relate to.

I feel that there is an appropriate, respectful and historically accurate way to describe LGBTQ+ historical figures, and that if we feel it is important to be sensitive in the terms we use for people who did not use those words for themselves, then we should be consistent in this approach. However, I also feel that it is not incorrect to look at someone who, for example, had relationships with people of the same and different genders and to acknowledge them as part of our bisexual+ cultural legacy. Their experiences will have had many differences to ours of course, but also some similarities.

The nature of bisexuality means that bisexual+ people are seen as not quite enough of either identity. Our histories are not represented in the heteronormative, heterosexual narrative, and are rarely acknowledged in lesbian and gay histories either. This is not surprising, as bisexual+ people often have to deal with having their identities being erased, depending on their partner at the time, but it raises issues when it comes to the process of representing or researching queer history. Any consideration or description of queer history needs to be aware of the nuance of describing historical LGB relationships, and also of describing historical relationships involving transgender, non-binary, or gender non-conforming people.

It is not possible to understand the histories of each letter of the LGBTQ+ umbrella separately. As we have already acknowledged, we are using modern words to understand the vast complexities of history across cultures and languages. For some, queer identity can be definitively divided into specific categories. I find it far more radical and freeing to consider that identity is more complicated than this, and that we are just doing our best with the words that we have now to express the wonderful complexities of our own identities in order to explain them to each other, to name our experiences, and to develop community.

For example, the word "lesbian" has historically been used to refer to the act of sex between two women, rather than something you could be or identify as (Solarz, 1999). The terms we use to understand ourselves are contemporary ways to understand something that crosses the boundaries of culture, language and time. That does not make these identities any less legitimate. We can assert the reality of LGBTQ+ history and celebrate it, while understanding that the distinctions we make now between lesbian, gay and bisexual+ identities did not exist until comparatively recently, and we can celebrate those distinctions in a way that does not eradicate the links between the two. Being more inclusive of bisexual+ people when discussing lesbian and gay history, and acknowledging that we are part of that historical narrative, does not diminish or exclude gay and lesbian people, but allows us to have a richer understanding of our histories and enriches our communities now.

The importance of being inclusive to bisexual+ people is clear when we look at the reality of life for many bisexual+ people. Studies have repeatedly found that bisexual+ people experience health disparities when compared to gay men, lesbians and heterosexual people. The Human Rights Campaign (HRC) report *Health Disparities among Bisexual People* (2015) found that bisexual people as a group face elevated risks of cancer, heart disease, sexually transmitted infections and poor mental health, as well as substance abuse, depression, self-harm and suicide attempts.

The HRC report also found that transgender people and people of colour form a large proportion of the bisexual+ community, which means these groups are even more vulnerable because of the intersections of biphobia, racism and transphobia. A study published in *Prevention Science* (Mereish, Sabra & Woulfe, 2017) found that the higher risk for bisexual+ people to experience anxiety, depression and suicidal thoughts is exacerbated because bisexual+ people feel as if they don't belong in any one community. This isolation limits their access to support and resources. Bisexual+ groups also receive much less funding and support than other LGBTQ+ organizations (Tichota, 2017), a problem which is further exacerbated by the fact that bisexual people experience discrimination from both heterosexual and lesbian and gay communities. Having evidence of the experiences of bisexual+ people is vital because it offers support to the lived experiences of individuals and the specific support and community they may benefit from.

Because of this, I think it is also important to look for joy in our histories, and there is one particular quote that first showed me the path to finding that joy. It's from June Jordan (2009), a

Caribbean-American poet, writer, teacher and bisexual and civil rights activist.

> Bisexuality means I am free and I am as likely to want to love a woman as I am likely to want to love a man, and what about that?
>
> Isn't that what freedom implies?
>
> If you are free, you are not predictable and you are not controllable.
>
> To my mind, that is the keenly positive, politicizing significance of bisexual affirmation...to insist upon the equal validity of all the components of social/sexual complexity.

Reading this was one of the first times that I'd looked at my sexuality as something to be proud of. As a bisexual person, I spend a lot of time and energy thinking about and analysing, debating and considering my identity, what I'm allowed to do and say, how much I'm allowed to claim my community's heritage. Instead of all that fear and anxiety, this quote told me that I can find joy in bisexuality. I feel lucky and excited by the engagement with my own identity that being bisexual encourages in me; I think about the ways I understand myself and the world around me because I've had to do that mental work, and I'm glad of that. As Jordan says, bisexuality is politicizing; it is freedom, it is not being predictable, it is not controllable. I summarize this quote to myself as simply "bisexuality is freedom" because to me bisexuality is liminal, difficult to define, complicated and therefore all the more wonderful. It is not entirely one thing, or another, instead it is its own complete identity. It means something different to everyone, but is still an identifier of community for me. And it invites me to challenge myself to think about who I am and what that means, and I couldn't be more grateful for that.

Another quote I find myself returning to is from a book called *Women and Bisexuality* by writer and activist Sue George (1993). I bought it from eBay, mostly because I liked the cover, and it ended up giving me a window into a powerful and vital history of bisexual+ activism and research in the UK that I found little representation of elsewhere. It also showed me that a lot of the debates I'd been having internally and with my peers, and that occur now on social media and online more generally, are often replicating debates the LGBTQ+ community has already had several times over. It reminded me that if we truly want to move forward, to build genuine and safe community for bisexual+ people in LGBTQ+ spaces, we need to look back as well as forward. As Sue George writes:

> Society controls people's sexuality by boxing them into categories of acceptable or unacceptable, the same or other.
>
> There is no place for bisexual in mainstream society...yet as we are not defined as "other" in the same way as people who exclusively seek same-sex relationships, lesbians and gay men can see us as "not oppressed"...
>
> Both straight and gay people have accused bisexuals of having the best of both worlds, presumably with the idea that bisexuals take only what is positive and pleasurable from different relationships and sexual identities, abandoning what is personally or politically difficult (p.21).

I particularly like what Sue says here about the false idea that bisexuals "take only what is positive and pleasurable from different relationships and sexual identities, abandoning what is personally or politically difficult". It helped me to realize that the internal questioning and fear that I felt a lot of the time was perhaps because of how others perceive bisexuality rather than an innate part of bisexuality itself. This, for me, is a major benefit of celebrating bisexual+ history; it helps us to better understand ourselves and to advocate for the rest of our community.

We can look to those who came before because despite the difficulty in finding them, there are many records of bisexual+ people and communities, including magazines, zines and publications created by and for the community. For example, *Anything That Moves* was a magazine for and by bisexual+ people which ran from 1990 to 2002. It was published by the San Francisco Bay Area Bisexual Network, as an expansion of Karla Rossi's newsletter. The title *Anything That Moves: Beyond the Myths of Bisexuality* was intended as a conscious reaction against this stereotype of bisexual people. Most of the issues were theme-based and attempted to represent the diverse range of voices and experiences within the bisexual+ community. Contributors did not have to declare their identity or label to be involved. You can read some of the articles included in the original magazine on the Anything That Moves website,[1] and I was recently able to purchase a few original copies of the magazine for the Bi History archive.

Another magazine I found in my research which shows that bisexual+ history exists outside a Western focus was *Anise*, a Japanese magazine for lesbian and bisexual women. A total of seven issues were published between 1996 and 1997 before it was temporarily suspended until 2001 for financial reasons. The first issue was titled *Anise for Womyn: for women who love*

---

1   https://anythingthatmovesarchive.carrd.co

women, and was then changed to specify that it was for lesbian and bisexual women. It included special features, three to five manga comics, short stories, reviews of books, movies, bars and events, personal advertisments, and a letters page, where readers could write in with their issues. These included letters from married women who were involved with other women looking for advice, lesbian and bisexual women who had feelings for straight friends, and other key issues. Much like *Anything That Moves*, *Anise* magazine provides a window into a community for queer women, and it was one that was explicitly inclusive of bisexual+ people.

Closer to my own home in Scotland, if we look at the programme of events for the Queens Crescent Club in Glasgow in February/March 1981, it includes an item for the Wednesday night meeting discussion: "On Bisexuality, Trend or Cop-out?" This small mention in their agenda shows that a discussion around whether bisexual+ people had a right to exist in LGBTQ+ spaces has been happening at least since the early 1980s, and yet continues to this day.

Even looking to the personal advertisements within records that may be considered (and solely identified as such by the archive or institutions) as only lesbian or gay can show a glimpse of bisexual+ people existing and thriving. From the *Pink Paper's*, Pink Personals, 9 February 1996: *"Bi Female, 30, would like to meet woman into computer surfing, cool + funky." "South East London Girl: bisexual, slim, attractive, blonde. Wishing to meet a companion for friendship, maybe more."* The *Pink Paper* was a UK newspaper covering queer issues, published by Millivres Prowler Limited. It was founded in 1987 and went online-only in 2009 before closing in 2012. During its life, it had a circulation in the tens of thousands across Britain and was distributed for free in bars, clubs, libraries and community centres.

It is vital that we celebrate and preserve bisexual+ history. I hope that my own work on the Bi History project has contributed to that, and am very proud of the work I have done and of the archive collection now held at the Bishopsgate Institute, which will hopefully support those undertaking research into bisexual+ history. I like to imagine that someone somewhere will visit the collection to learn more about themselves, get to experience (as I did) that moment where you hold a piece of your community's history in your hands, and know the relief and peace of finding that you are just another part of a long history of bisexual+ people.

I still sometimes see people responding to discussion of bisexual+ history as though it somehow it detracts from the history of lesbian and gay communities if it is named as such. I hope that we can all reach a point where we can celebrate the joyous complexities of LGBTQ+ history as a whole and that acknowledging the potential for something to be part of the history of the bisexual+ community only enriches its value.

I hope more bisexual+ people are able to see the value in the records we create ourselves of our history, so that someone else someday might come across a flyer for a club night or a zine we've made, and find a sense of community through coming into contact with it. I also hope that my work will encourage people to be more aware of the function of archives in our societies. We do not have to solely rely on institutions and the rules they prescribe to preserve our own history of our community if we do not want to. I want us to consider the importance of our own records of our lives and activism, and also to demand more of any institution or collection that purports to represent the LGBTQ+ community if it is not representing the reality of the existence of the bisexual+ community.

References

Delaram, R.K. (2019). "Invisible majority: Bisexual people seeking asylum 'not worthy of belief'." The Oxford Research Centre in the Humanities, 26 June 2019. www.torch.ox.ac.uk/article/invisible-majority-bisexual-people-seeking-asylum-not-worthy-of-belief.

Diamond, L.M. (2008). Female bisexuality from adolescence to adulthood: Results from a 10-year longitudinal study. *Developmental Psychology*, 44(1), 5–14.

George, S. (1993). *Women and Bisexuality*. London: Scarlet Press.

Human Rights Campaign. (2015). *Health Disparities among Bisexual People*. www.hrc.org/resources/health-disparities-among-bisexual-people.

Jordan, J. (2009). "A New Politics of Sexuality" in *Some Of Us Did Not Die* (eBook edition). London: Civitas Books.

Mereish, E.H., Sabra, L.K.W. & Woulfe, J. (2017). Bisexual-specific minority stressors, psychological distress, and suicidality in bisexual individuals: The mediating role of loneliness. *Prevention Science*, 18(6), 716–725.

Solarz, A.L. (ed.) (1999). *Lesbian Health: Current Assessment and Directions for the Future*. Washington, DC: National Academy Press.

Steinmetz, K. (2020). "What does 'pansexual' mean? Behind the rise of the word." Time, 7 January 2020. https://time.com/5760209/what-pansexual-means.

Tichota, N. (2017). "Bisexual discrimination." Medium, 7 November 2017. https://medium.com/@nicktichota/bisexual-discrimination-e762e46fb2f.

CHAPTER 2

Looping Around and Spinning Out

Marcus Morgan

Marcus Morgan (they/them) founded The Bisexual Index and The Bisexual Underground, co-founded SM Bisexuals, chaired the London Bisexual Group, was chief organizer of three national bisexual conventions and of one international bisexual conference. Marcus is a Stonewall Role Model, a government-listed bisexuality champion, the UK's only known "bisexual activist magician" and is very tired (of biphobia).

He just said, "Hello my name is Jeff and I'm bisexual," and then he burst into tears in front of a room full of men. And that was when I realized what I had to do.

Doggett's Coat and Badge is not a quaint old pub. It's a concrete tower on the banks of the Thames that is named after the founder of the London Bridge to Chelsea rowing race, known colloquially as the Oxford/Cambridge boat race because *somehow* it's always those two teams in the race.

It has a lovely view of the river, of course, and is close enough to tube and rail stations, but what was important in the early

2000s was that it had underused function rooms and it didn't really know how to price them at weekends.

My friend Katy and I had previously organized a "meet the bi+ community" event called BiFest at a place called the London Activist Resource Centre. BiFest was intended as a gentle introduction to the idea of rooms full of bi+ people, somewhere to dip your toe before diving into the pool of somewhere like a monthly group or a big event like BiCon.

Don't get me wrong – highly immersive spaces are awesome and there's nothing like having several hundred bisexuals wash over you. As it were. But it can be very intimidating at first. And a Saturday daytime event is more accessible to people who don't want to explain to their friends where they were on a Friday night, or tell their partners where they're going for a weekend.

As there was a gap in the timetable that called for it, I agreed to run "Coming Out for Bisexual Men". Piece of cake, I said. Have it and eat it. No worries. I'd been facilitating session discussions for years and years. There'd be no surprises.

I was wrong.

It was mid-afternoon on a sunny spring Saturday. A lot of the people in the building were old friends who had come along just to have the chance to see each other and be in a "bisexual is normal" space. Others I knew peripherally, but delightfully there were plenty of people I'd never seen at a bi+ event ever before and so I was pretty sure had never engaged with or found the bi+ community before. The session came round; it was in the second or third slot so we'd all already been to "What is Bisexuality Anyway?", or ignored it and been at the bar.

Big room, lots of friendly faces. To be entirely honest I'd sort of half tuned the discussion out. After a decade in the bi+ movement I was very used to workshops that started with everyone in a circle telling us their names and where they were from, and trying to keep it short so maybe ha ha an animal that starts with the same letter (otherwise everyone's life story meant the introduction could take up half the allotted time). The man next to me had listened to each person's introduction and life snippets as we went round the circle, with admiration, with respect, at times with horror. When it was his turn he said, "My name is Jeff and I'm a bisexual man but..." and then he burst into tears.

There was a moment of shocked surprise and then he was getting a hug from someone and a tissue, and reassurances that it was okay to do that and no he was not being silly. When he'd recovered he explained that he'd known he was bisexual since he was a teenager.

This was emotional for him because it was the first time he'd felt safe enough to tell people he was bisexual. And what it had taken for him to feel that safety was a room of fellow bisexual men, at a bisexual event.

But what made me realize we need to talk urgently about the things no one talks about was one detail about the timing.

Jeff explained he had known since he was a teenager when he first read the word "bisexual" in the dictionary.

He had wanted to tell his school friends but feared bullying.

He had wanted to come out at university but the "gay soc" was clearly not going to be supportive.

He had wanted to come out to his partner, his wife, but had been scared of the potential reaction.

He wanted to tell people. He wanted to feel supported and seen, and find other people like him. But he hadn't until that day. He finally felt safe to tell someone, and it was us. For the first time.

Aged 65.

I was already giving talks about "being bisexual" but the more I thought about his story the more I realized we needed to change the way we talk about the meaning of the word "bisexual". It is a word bisexual people are happy to use to describe themselves to each other. But away from such friendly faces are we still "saying" we are bisexual, or are we "admitting" it? How had a word with such a simple dictionary definition become apparently shameful? Why was it a confession, why was it a secret? Would it be easier to tell people we're bi if they understood what the word meant, and didn't mean? People might not be intentionally gatekeeping us, but perhaps they've left their baggage in our doorway...

I love change. I'm a huge fan of saying, "You know what, let's chuck that out and try a different way!" I keep doing it myself. I was a gay teenager, then became bisexual aged 21. I realized I was non-binary when I was 25 and tried to come out but then kept a lid on it until I was much older. I'd worked in offices doing administrative jobs all my life, and then aged 43 I became a full-time magician.

So I've always thought change is good. Evolution is good. And being pro-change I wanted to look at the message the bi+ community was transmitting about bisexuality – about who was bisexual and who wasn't, about who was "allowed to call themselves bisexual".

A few years before that discussion I had first seen and fallen in love with the bisexual pride flag. Three horizontal stripes: wide magenta, narrower purple, wide blue. It was breathtakingly simple, and came quite quickly on the heels of the rainbow flag. The colours came from a "bi triangles" symbol which had overlapping pink and blue triangles created by Liz Nania, making a purple triangular intersection. And although the flat horizontal bars diluted the idea of intersection, they did bring one great strength that many of the more modern flag designs, and updates to flags, seem to have moved away from.

It wasn't a symbol, with lines or shapes, and needing someone to draw it. It was a sequence. One, two, three.

There had been attempts at universal bisexual symbols before, but they were complicated. Some were gender symbols in various combinations but they were not widely understood and often the configurations implied multiple relationships. They specified specific genders too. It was the turn of the century (I can say that but do realize I mean 1999–2000, I'm not that old) and we were moving away from using words like "both". It had been a useful word, useful shorthand, but a wider understanding of gender diversity had arrived.

The rainbow Pride flag was first unveiled in 1978. That seems like forever, but it only came into common usage very slowly. It had eight stripes, each with a distinct meaning when Gilbert Baker designed it. But by the time it became popular enough to attract the notice of mainstream merchandisers most people seeing it just thought of it as a pretty set of colours. Big manufacturers got on the bandwagon and had handy stocks of fabric with fewer stripes, so why not make it with fewer? It's still a rainbow, still a gay thing. First it dropped down to seven and then six. Effectively pink and turquoise were dropped by capitalism – "sex" and "magic". Says it all really!

Mike Page designed the bi pride flag in 1998. Three stripes, simpler – harder to get wrong. And crucially not of equal size and not of incredibly distinct colours. The purple in the middle he deliberately chose to be close in hue to both the pink and the blue. He did not intend originally for those colours to represent genders. They were not "men and women" – they were, he said, the different kinds of attractions. If you've heard a definition of the bi in bisexual meaning the two of "both same sex and different sex attraction" then that marries with the flag. That purple stripe is the intersection between both attraction to those like us, and those unlike us. Of course, the idea that the bi+ community is where the straight people meet the gay people can sometimes be quite the harmful stereotype!

When I was growing up I heard words in the playground that were used as slurs and I went home and asked my parents and then checked the dictionary with a sore ear. There were all sorts of fascinating words in the dictionary, even in the 1970s. In the dictionary, bisexual was defined as "sexually attracted by both men and women" and I remember thinking that didn't sound so bad. Later, as a teenager, I was certain I was gay but for some reason the idea that bi was something bad had never taken root.

The dictionary definition is crap though, and I can't tell you how many times people bring it up as if the dictionary is an immutable law that prescribes how future generations must zealously speak. It's not. It's a tar pit into which words stumble when they're already tired and then they fossilize. It's a record of what words used to mean. You can't capture "now".

First off, "sexual attraction" is dated. What about romantic? What about social? Next, "attracted by" sounds somehow off, and it's only when you turn it over in your mind a few times that you realize you want to say "attracted to", because these days we don't see attraction as something other people do to us, their unwitting pawns! It's not a passive force you exert – my attraction is mine and it's up to me to choose what to do with it.

And more obviously, "both men and women". Aside from the wider understanding we have of gender these days, even in the 1970s the dictionary didn't say that straight meant "attracted to men if you're a woman and women if you're a man". It left what the gender was open, but noted it was the opposite, the reflection, the opposing team. All very adversarial, very us-and-them, but still!

Why had it taken Jeff so long to tell other people he was a bisexual man? The more I thought about it, the more I started to realize – people weren't talking about bisexuality because they didn't know how to. Bisexual erasure was such that in addition to not considering that people like me even existed, most people didn't have a toolkit to discuss it, or useful handy words to explain it.

We knew the dictionary was wrong, but without an alternative we couldn't easily say why. In the early 2000s, lots of people were saying bisexuality could not even be defined. On their webpages, Stonewall used to say, "a changeable sexual orientation in which gender may or may not be a factor". If it's hard to say what it is, then it's hard to say that you're it, so you're probably wrong, and there's probably not any more of you, so say you're gay for political reasons and don't let the side down.

Bisexuality is confusing, so you're confused. So shut up because you cannot know what you're talking about.

And we did shut up. We kept quiet. When people asked us if we were gay we'd say yes or "Yes, I'm bisexual". LGBT Pride Month only exists because a bisexual woman, a kinky polyamorous bisexual woman called Brenda Howard thought that "Pride" was a good word for the events and it should be more than just a protest, it should be a celebration.

But we kept quiet. We kept our heads down. That's why on our flag Mike chose a shade of purple that blends in to the pink and the blue – because there's a dual meaning. The colours also represent the communities, gay and straight, and the way bisexual people are present in both, but not fully acknowledged in either.

I first saw the flag and knew it was going to be really useful only a few months after its debut. BiNet USA's president of the time credits me, I found out a couple of years ago, with popularizing it in the UK and Europe. But when I saw it I knew it was going to be great for the exact same reason the rainbow flag is better than the Union Jack. It's not a complex symbol, it's an incredibly simple pattern. So I took the collection of lines I saw on the fledgling bi flag website and just started using it everywhere!

Pink, purple, blue. It's a coded message to the person looking for the bi group meeting in the bar or the food hall. Pink, purple, blue – you can create the pattern in candles, or stripes on a wall, or bracelets, or hairstyles, or...anything. It's visibility for people who know what it is and it's not a threat to anyone who doesn't know. It's safety.

We see ourselves in it, just as we need to see ourselves in role models, in the press, in movies and TV...and in the dictionary.

There was a session at BiCon in 2007, I think, about the future of bi+ activism in the UK, about how to move forward. I was on the panel as someone who had organized previous events, and who had already volunteered to run future ones.

The conversation was wide ranging and a lot of it was navel gazing. It would be fair to say a lot of the rest of it was "wouldn't it be great if" discussions about what we could do if the mythological funder ever graced a bi activist with several thousand pounds.

But one of the elements stuck with me; it was a thing I'd brought up. We didn't have an organization, or structure, that wasn't geared towards either running a specific event or publishing a specific periodical. There was no British Bisexual Society.

That there could be, maybe even should be, wasn't a new idea. Someone had tried it in the 1990s and suggested their new organization would *run* bi groups, publish newsletters, be an overarching umbrella that all bi+ people in the UK would sign up to.

The thing I'd said though that was different this time was this: the group could be for creating resources, things that people could opt to use. It could be a lobbying group. A group could have a very specific purpose that wasn't currently being done, and so not duplicate anyone's tireless efforts.

Of course, as the discussion continued the room full of bisexuals first decided we'd need two groups, and then possibly more than two. Sometimes the stereotypes are true. One group to be like Outrage, one like Stonewall. One all angry and punk, the other all reasonable and wearily explanatory.

There was of course no real reason why their members wouldn't overlap. Or even their leadership.

And then we started talking about numbers, and structures, and how many people might like to work on a constitution for the organization, and how hard is it to found a charity. Then the workshop timed out, and everyone wanted to get off to the Naked Picnic or go and discuss Bisexuality in Science Fiction, so we all said we'd come back to it next year. Because there was no way to have the discussion outside BiCon and still include all the people who had been at that event.

The idea stuck with me though. What if there was an organization specifically to tackle one thing? What would that thing be?

And then I met Jeff, and realized what it would be.

By the time of that BiFest the community had largely moved away from the dictionary definition of bisexual and had been for years using slogans like "fancy men, fancy women, fancy both". There was no universally accepted, or suggested, alternative though. People felt we didn't need one. BiCon made it a point of pride, saying the event was there to discuss what being bisexual meant to people, not tell them. BiNet over in the USA had "a person whose enduring physical, sexual, romantic and/ or emotional attraction is to other people of various sexes and/ or gender identities", which tries to pad itself out into inclusion.

But the lack of agreement was frequently used against us. If, when asked, one hundred bisexual people all gave different answers, then that was seen as proof that even bisexuals can't agree what the word means. Of course, the issue is in part about how you ask the question. Ask a hundred cat lovers what a cat is, to them, and you'll get answers about companionship and beating loneliness, and feline grace, and ingenuity, and so on. Some may even mention the memes on the internet, or Garfield, and so on. Few will say "a cat is a small domesticated carnivore, *Felis domestica* or *Felis catus*, bred in a number of varieties", like a dictionary. But that doesn't mean there's no understanding of what cats are or that nothing can call itself a cat. They just haven't bothered to start from absolute basics because they have taken it as read that the word reflects a common and self-explanatory concept.

What if, I wondered, we had a definition that people could see themselves reflected in. That people could recognize as applying to them, and which was clear. Not academic language, not a long paragraph of justifying yourself, nothing that would be out of place in answer to the question, "So Jeff, I heard you're bisexual. What's all that about?" in a pub. Plain English and, importantly, as short as possible. If the answer to "Why did you say you were gay?" can be as simple as "Yeah, well, I only fancy men," then couldn't there be an equally simple version for bisexuality too?

And wouldn't that be a fantastic thing to have an organization promote? Wouldn't that be a fantastic thing to create an organization to promote?

Having that definition would be a great tool for activism. A website with a good frequently asked questions section to go with it could also be really handy. All the stupid questions we get asked could be on there, with reusable answers.

All that was then needed was to find the definition and start the org.

Back when the first indoor bans on smoking in commercial venues came in there was often a couple of spokespeople who would turn up on the television news from the two sides of the debate. One group was "defending smokers' rights", the other was "concerned for smokers' health". And much like the more quirky Christian groups that sometimes pop up, they each only appeared to have one spokesperson. That's okay – media training isn't common. A quick look at their websites would, however, turn up the lovely phrase as an answer to the question of joining and membership. We are not, they said, a membership organization but we do welcome donations.

No members. What if rather than being Random Guy Who Wants to Talk to Local Pride about their Lack of Bisexual Inclusion, one was Guy From Bisexual Organization That Just Happens Not To Have Members?

Certainly I was finding it harder to make people listen to me about bisexuality as Marcus Morgan from BiCon, But Not This Year's BiCon But A Previous Year's BiCon.

Sometimes it's easier to just do it, to make a move, take a step forward, see what happens later. Run it, as they say, up the flagpole and see if the cat laps it up. So I wrote the shortest definition of bisexual I could.

Rather than trying to make it more inclusive by adding clauses and footnotes, I made it inclusive by taking words away. Not attracted by, not both, in fact I removed the concept of "two" altogether. For all the faults it has, the dictionary definition didn't include "equally" or "in the same way" or "at the same time". So there was no need to put in any clause against those. It always felt a bit like when a magician describes an envelope as a "perfectly ordinary" envelope. Don't run, the maxim goes, when you're not being chased.

"Bisexuality," I wrote, "is attraction to more than one gender." That definition is as simple as it can be. It includes people who think there are two genders. It includes people who know there are more. It includes (and I've met them, but hadn't thought of it at the time) people who wouldn't go as far as two, but mainly one and a bit of the other, non-integer genders. More than one gender.

I had the purpose, and, yes, I could start the organization without other members. If there were no other members, no one needed to see a constitution immediately or ask for the bank details yet. In 2009, I was waiting for a train at Vauxhall when I finished the list in my notebook of potential names for the organization with "The Bisexual Index". Next morning, I registered the website and started a Twitter (now known as X) account.

Now there are over thirty thousand followers on X for the account, Stonewall uses the "Index Definition" and it has spread across the world.

Everything was going well, but the results were taking up a lot of my spare time. I was being asked by organizations to run sessions about bisexuality because now I was Marcus from The Bisexual Index. In the course of a year I headed up the BiCon in 2010, which was also the International Conference on Bisexuality, got married, welcomed my son into the world, moved house, got most of the way through 2011 and then became mentally ill, signed off as unfit for my day job, and was then fired in 2012.

I was screaming on the rollercoaster, but not because I wanted it to go faster.

By the time I was tearfully accepting a three-month sick note from my doctor I was desperate. I had long seen myself as being my work role, and all the activism and hobbies as being garnish or accents. I was an office worker who also did bisexual activism. I was not a bisexual activist who funded their work through a day job. My identity crumbled as depression and anxiety took hold. If they'd give me another chance I'd figured I'd stop all side stuff, dedicate myself to being the very best employee I could. My nose would be all over that grindstone.

Looking back, I'm now glad they didn't give me another chance. It's taken the best part of the ten years since to realize that, and to stop my brain spiralling into "what ifs" about how I could have begged them to keep me. To keep bullying me and exploiting me.

I've never met a bi+ activist without mental health issues of some sort. When we encounter prejudice, even if we're somewhat inured to it, it wears down the barriers. But people just look at the final straw and wonder why the camel is making such a scene.

I went to the job centre. They were as sympathetic as they could be. You've had your previous post for 13 years, they noted, and were fired for...

A rustle of notes, and a sigh. On paper the reason I left was "gross misconduct". I had tried to take my employers to a tribunal but didn't have the paper trail to prove it was mental-health discrimination. There's no way you'll get a job in another office with that. Is there anything else you can do?

Well, I said, yes. A couple of things – but I'm not sure which would be a better money maker, and I have no idea how to be self-employed.

Ah, they said, eyes lighting up, we can get you on training courses to be self-employed, and that gets you off the unemployment figures. You can claim New Enterprise Allowance, which is the same amount but with an expiry date.

So tell us, what can you do? There was, I said, two things.

In 1992, when I first became a regular at the London Bisexual Group I was quickly pressed into service as someone who could do announcements at the start of meetings. From there, I found myself facilitating group discussions, often from a place of relative ignorance of the specific subject because the role was to keep the conversation going and ensure that people had a chance to speak. From there, I ended up on the committee, and then became the chairperson. All of it public speaking experience.

I'd never have believed I could do it when I was a teenager. I spent my life trying to be invisible and denying that I'd been sent to speech therapy classes to deal with my communication issues. But by the time I needed the new job I had a wealth of experience talking to people about bisexuality, and a lifetime of lived experience. That might not be the money spinner I needed though, and that was where the second string to my bow came in.

A year before, when I was first signed off on mental health grounds, I had decided I needed to do something about the doom spirals of thoughts that continued to drag me down, that kept me trapped in endless re-runs of the conversations and confrontations I had had with my bosses. I needed something else to think about.

I went to a magic shop in London and bought a book on card tricks. I moved my work pass out of my coat pocket and put the cards in there. Brushing against them in my pocket became a constant reminder – I wasn't an office worker who did activism and magic. I was an activist and magician, who had (albeit for not much longer) a day job.

And so I set out on two different trains. On one I was Magic Marcus, children's magician. On the other I was Marcus Morgan from The Bisexual Index, activist. It took a few years for the tracks to converge, but the crash was fabulous fun.

As part of the activism side of things I went on Stonewall's role models training, a special session catering to members of the bi+ community. How, we were asked, could we bring our whole selves to work? How could we stand out in the workplace as bisexual role models? This got me thinking, how could I do this as someone who was self-employed? Obviously the public speaking was all about me being bisexual, but none of the magic was. Could it be possible to combine the two?

In early 2016, I attempted it for the first time with a card trick I threw into a talk I was doing on bi+ issues for an LGBT forum. I felt it went down surprisingly well. I decided to theme more magic towards a bisexual message; I made my debut at Coventry Pride and then went to BiCon with a fledgling bisexual magic act. That year's BiCon was having a cabaret night, hosted by a member of the organizing team who was apparently an experienced stand-up comedian. It was, dear reader, a disaster.

The UK National Conference on Bisexuality/Bisexual Convention, aka BiCon, is a bubble. Necessarily a bubble, a wonderful bubble. It's certainly not the same kind of atmosphere as comedy night down your local straight pub. The host's compering did not go well. Afterwards he was confused, because jokes about Jimmy Saville, trans people, bestiality and BDSM (bondage, dominance, sadism and masochism) had all gone down brilliantly at other venues.

By the interval, he was being talked to in a corner and I was approached by the organizing team's leader to ask if I'd take over for the second half.

On the way home I looked at the three tricks I'd done and

asked myself, "What if we had a bi+ cabaret but it wasn't at Bi-Con? Not just bisexual people performing, but acts that centred bisexuality?"

A month later I realized there wasn't a Bi Visibility Day event in London that I fancied the look of, and another magician on Facebook mentioned a local pub with a stage that was looking to host for free events to fill gaps in their diary.

And so "an evening of the bisexual variety" CaBiRet was born. It's still going strong, twice a year apart from during global pandemics. Who knows how many of those there will have been by the time you read this! CaBiRet provides an opportunity for a bi+ audience to see something they so seldom can – their own reflection in the mirror that culture holds up to society. Since the start, I've prioritized intersectional voices and worked to keep the line-ups relevant to the community as it is today.

When I was in speech therapy as a child, I never dreamed I'd speak to crowds of thousands. When I was in my teens, I never dreamed I'd still be alive in my fifties. When I was trapped in an office, I never dreamed I'd be a magician. When I first joined the bi+ community, I never dreamed I'd become a leader.

I could have had those dreams. Society weighs on people from minorities to "be realistic" with their hopes, their ambitions.

Fuck that.

Dream it!

CHAPTER 3

Bodies of Knowledge

Bisexual Men and Sexual Violence

Tanaka Mhishi

Tanaka Mhishi (he/him) is an author, playwright and performer whose works with issues surrounding masculinity and trauma have been produced on screen by the BBC and on stages nationwide. His theatrical work includes This Is How It Happens, a play about male survivors of sexual violence, and the Off West End Award-nominated Boys Don't, which he co-wrote and performed in partnership with Papertale Productions and Half Moon Theatre. Tanaka is a trustee for SurvivorsUK, a charity supporting male and non-binary survivors of sexual violence in London and across the UK. His first book, Sons and Others: On Loving Male Survivors, a new look at how men navigate life after sexual violence, was published in late 2022 by 404Ink.

When did you know you were bi?

That long summer between GCSEs and A-levels, that's when I knew I was bisexual. It was as if my body sensed freedom and decided to run full tilt towards it. My mother took me to Sri Lanka to see her father and stepmother.

My body does well in Sri Lanka. My hair behaves. My joints are loose. I remember letting the shower water shimmy down my stomach, and laughing as I put cream across my nose. I cried so much that summer, mostly in the shower. Mostly out of relief.

When we got back to London I had a new haircut and got my first tailored suit and I was ready to fall in love.

His name was Oliver. We slept next to each other at a mutual friend's sleepover and in the middle of the night he whispered, "Turn round" into my neck. I did. He kissed me. The next morning we pretended nothing had happened. Around us, our friends put on a movie, and we casually contrived to be seated next to each other, sharing a blanket.

He took out his phone and texted me: *Last night was fun. :)*

Be cool, I thought, be cool. Don't fuck it up. My reply was noncommittal, but I slid a smile across the sofa. The rest of the sleepover party were watching *Mean Girls*.

Do you want to see me again? he texted. I suspected that my heart was thumping so loudly it might destabilize the building. I composed my reply carefully: *Sure, if you want to see me?*

Cool. Noncommittal. Pretend you couldn't care less.

He tapped away at his phone for approximately seven eternities. I waited to see his reply. And waited some more. Empires rose and fell. Planets formed. Species evolved. Regina George got hit by a bus.

At last, his response dropped into my inbox: *Of course! You're amazing. Are we on then? :)*

I nodded, forgetting myself. Nobody noticed except him.

I felt his hand slip into mine under the blanket. We carefully didn't look at each other, and I sank down, hiding my smile behind my knees.

We were together for just over a year.

He was complicated, intense, musical, and most importantly

he chose me. *Me*, with my NHS glasses and spots and puffball hair. Who wouldn't fall in love? I had spent such a long time resigned to my own loneliness that I think I would have fallen for him no matter how he treated me.

It would end horribly; him callous and deceitful, me self-righteous and overdramatic. But for a long while it was good. He was kind and I was keen.

The second week we were together he took me up to the lake at our school and we found a patch of wood where we couldn't be seen. It was November, and his lips were cold. I remember my fingers on a button somewhere and the smell of him; synthetic lemon and hair gel. We fed each other words between the kisses and I remember touching him over his trousers. There. Proof. Not just in his hardness, but in the little involuntary thrust and shudder that went through his body. I was not ugly. I was not unlovable.

More than comfort; this was a thrill.

I know, I know, a 17-year-old's erection is not the healthiest or most reliable measure of self-worth. And yet, standing in that clutch of trees with my first real lover trembling under my touch, I mattered. I had evidence in my hand. And it felt good.

"You can suck it if you want?"

I hesitated.

"Only if you want to." He moved himself backwards slightly, to give me space to make my decision. I knew he was more experienced than me, and he was careful not to cajole me. The moment he began to withdraw my body made the decision. The phrase "enthusiastic consent" doesn't even begin to cover it; I nearly combusted. I pulled him flush against me, let him kiss me. If you've ever sung and nailed a perfect note you will know how this felt; this vibrating rightness. My knees hit the leaf litter.

Bisexuality slows sex down. You cannot assume, for example,

that penises like to be touched in this way or that way. That clitorises will want this amount or that amount of pressure. And you certainly can't assume that the people who have them will want to be loved in the same way as each other. You have to take it body by body.

That was always the thrill of a new lover to me; a new person with new pleasure points to learn, and on their own terms.

But the body of knowledge of bisexual men is confined to the site of its birth; it exists between cotton sheets, not printed ones. As I tried to research this chapter, to reach beyond my own experience, I found that most of the writing about us is more concerned with public health than with pleasure. These are the questions that the academic world wants to answer about bisexual men: Are we really gay? Are we good husbands to straight women or bad ones? Do we exist at all?

Above all, are we an HIV risk?

I shiver when I find the reams of research dedicated to this question. Not because it's not a worthwhile question, but because it's all people seem to want to know about us. And sometimes that need to know can turn violent.

Dani and I got on immediately; she was the kind of cheery which looks effortless, with a wicked sense of humour and huge, expressive eyes. We talked about Disney villains, walked along the seafront. Her boyfriend Paul hung back with the rest of the guys as we made our way to the club. I'd noticed his eye on me earlier, and taken the precaution of mentioning an ex-boyfriend earlier in the evening. I knew he'd assume I was gay and, in my circles, that meant he'd leave me alone to talk to his girlfriend in peace.

Did I like her? Was I flirting? Perhaps. We got on in that easy way which could easily pass a hundred Sunday afternoons without getting bored. We connected, that much I knew.

I remember thinking that Paul was extremely dull, that she must be bored out of her mind with a monosyllabic, strait-laced, unadventurous guy like him. That she could do a lot better if she'd only...

Oh.

Alright. I liked her.

We got to the club and Paul barged ahead to escort her in. Dani rolled her eyes and we smiled at each other.

We danced a lot, all of us. We drank a bit; my memories of the night are sort of sharp and splintered, which means I was teetering on the edge of sensible consumption.

We weren't too close to each other, I know that. I was being careful. There was at least a hand's breadth between us. Even under the arches of the seaside club, in the purple light and with the BPM a certain kind of dangerous, I knew the rules. I knew that touching her, or allowing her to touch me, would be too much.

I remember that there was a moment where her eyes were looking up at me. I remember the way she was rocking slightly against the bench she was sitting on. I remember the way she smelled. And I remember the feel of her finger, suddenly touching mine.

It would have made so much sense to take her hand. Just for a moment. Just to see what happened next.

Paul tore across the dance floor. Dani and I looked up at him as he barrelled towards us, his face livid.

He grabbed me – I want to say by the scruff of my shirt but it was more like my shoulder. I remember a button pressing into my clavicle, I remember my back hitting the brickwork. I remember Dani there, on the margins, making these sort of worried, upset noises that must have been words. I remember feeling his hands scrabble for a proper grip, and knowing that if he could get one of them free, he would rabbit punch me, swift and vicious. And I remember what he said:

"PEOPLE LIKE YOU ARE THE REASON INNOCENT WOMEN GET AIDS!"

His hand snapped back to punch me.

"People like you." Bisexual men. The worst type of queer boys because they're the ones who can steal your girlfriend. And – if the evidence is anything to go by – straight men should be worried about bisexual guys.

Australian academic Maria Pallotta-Chiarolli (2015) found that many straight women in relationships with openly bisexual men had better sex, more equitable home lives and more fulfilling experiences as mothers than women with straight husbands and boyfriends.

She also found that being with a queer partner pulls straight women into the no-man's land. They exist slightly outside straightness, but not quite within the queer community – a place where bisexual people in different gender relationships often find themselves. They might be women attracted to men, but if bisexual men's queerness is contagious, they were positioned as having "caught" it, and that came with a certain amount of shaming from the outside world.

For some straight women and the straight men around them, this is intolerable. In 2020, a Spanish man was successfully sued by his ex-wife for €10,000 for "moral and emotional damages" for not disclosing his bisexuality. The couple had divorced ten years earlier, but Javier Vilalta found himself the subject of the lawsuit which claimed she would never have married him if she had been aware of his sexuality. The case was overturned on appeal in 2021 (Browning, 2021), but the initial decision shows just how easy it is for bi+ men to be punished for being open about their identities.

So maybe it's not really HIV that Paul was scared about his girlfriend catching from me. We were, after all, just talking. Maybe it was queerness itself.

Plus, if you're a straight man whose girlfriend leaves you for a queer guy...well, what does that say about your masculinity?

Paul's punch never landed; some other men nearby pulled him off me. The bouncers must have seen him and sensed trouble because they bundled us both off the dance floor moments later.

Technically, I suppose, it was a hate crime, but it was one too subtle to explain there and then and so it went unpunished. This is often how biphobia and biphobic violence works, resting on top of other associated prejudices like a circus performer balancing on their fellows. The bouncers decided we were "fighting over a girl" and booted us both out of the club. No questions asked.

It's a little trite, but this kicking out is a good metaphor for how authorities deal with violence against bisexual people. Out on the seafront I watched, waiting in the dark of the promenade arch for Paul and Dani to get a safe distance away. We are dealt with only as risks to be managed.

At 18, I was technically homeless for six months. I say "technically" because I had lots of advantages: friends with spare rooms, a middle-class accent, teachers who were willing to go to bat for me, a free travel card for the buses. I did very little rough sleeping and it was summer. But at one point I lived in a youth hostel, which the landlord had taken care to fill with young queer men. I shared a dorm with an emaciated, silent American who looked as if he had been through a homophobic hell, and a man from Tenerife who was in London to have as much sex as he could.

The landlord focused on me immediately. I was the youngest,

the poorest, the brownest. It started with "accidental" brushing against me in the corridors or at the breakfast bar.

"How long have you known you're gay?" he asked.

"I'm bi," I said, automatically.

"Ah. Nice and kinky then?" he said.

I told him I was seeing someone, hoping he would leave me alone. He did not.

"She doesn't count."

From the moment he knew I was bi, the harassment escalated. He told me how much I reminded him of his "little Bangladeshi boyfriends", called me into his room while he was in his underwear and offered to take some money off the rent if I had sex with him. He goaded the boys I was sharing a room with to try and "convince" me to be all the way gay.

Near the end of August, I woke up with someone else's erection pressing into my back. I remember being icy calm, then the panic mounting as I felt his hand moving towards my crotch.

I managed to laugh it off, to not-so-subtly make enough noise protesting to wake the others in the room. Embarrassed, he climbed over me and staggered back to bed. I began my plans to leave right then and there. I would have too, except that the London riots started.

Quickly, various areas around the country were going up in flames and the police were prowling the streets. Growing up Black in London, I'd already been questioned aggressively by the police for such suspicious activity as *running for the bus* (I might have stolen something), *waiting for the bus* (loitering) and *sketching in public* (suspicion of terrorism). In the moment, it seemed safer to stay inside with the sex offenders than risk the Metropolitan Police.

I waited it out, being careful and tactful, sneaking naps rather than sleeping properly. By the time I could get away I was so sleep-deprived that I filed the sexual assaults away with the summer's other hardships and moved on to my next challenge.

Years later, when I was researching sexual violence against men for my master's degree, I came across a study which found that 47 per cent of bisexual men had experienced some form of sexual assault (Frieden, Thomas R., et al., 2012).

I was sitting in the St Peter's Library in Brighton when I first read that statistic, and I remember staring so hard at the screen I could see individual pixels. It felt very, very personal. And I had questions.

Why us? At whose hands?

But that's where the trail went cold. No one had thought that statistic was important enough to warrant a body of knowledge on what was behind it.

Instead, we have endless studies which ask, "Do bisexual men exist?", most of which involve hooking (cis) bi men's penises up to machines to measure their tumescence (Jabbour et al., 2020). Reading these studies, I cannot help but feel an echo of the way I was touched in the youth hostel – as an object of curiosity, as a challenge, as a problem to solve.

Similarly, when I read yet another hand-wringing article about bisexual men as the ultimate HIV transmission vectors I can't help but feel as if I am being pinned against the wall by another version of Paul and interrogated about whether or not I am a threat to these "innocent women" whom I must, of course, be deceiving.

What would it cost for the world to be curious about bi+ men and how we experience the world?

Here's a hypothesis for you: the costs would be far outweighed by the gains.

In her famous TED Talk (2011) and book *Men, Women and Worthiness* (2013), the researcher Brené Brown deftly summarizes our unwillingness to sit with men's complex inner lives. She writes that "from the very earliest tender age I think the message for boys is 'it doesn't matter what's happening behind that curtain. You need to project [an image of being] always knowing, all powerful, always great, all the time.'"

Brown and her colleagues' research reveals a common theme about how our society prefers to think of men and men's sexuality as simple. We like to think we know men's sexuality; they are gay or straight, visually motivated, unemotional, unchanging and innate and at least tending towards the aggressive. I have always found it deeply disturbing that my rapist's sexual conduct is seen as unequivocally male. We all condemn sexual offences, and many people are comfortable saying, given the disproportionate number of male perpetrators, that sexual violence has something to say about manhood and vice versa. On the other hand, male survivors are seen as exceptions. Our experiences – when they are mentioned – are not held to have any real bearing on the way male sexuality functions in our world beyond our own bedrooms.

Elsewhere, I have written about the philosophical violence that rape and abuse enact; the way it cuts us off from certain pools of knowledge – a form of what philosophers call epistemic injustice. Those cut off cannot draw from the pool of collective understanding, in this case understanding about male sexuality, nor are their experiences seen as legitimate contributions to that same pool.

A quick perusal of outlets like *Men's Health*, which have longstanding sexual health advice sections and advice columns, shows a number of injunctions to stop men from participating in or upholding rape culture, suggesting that writers and editors view potential perpetrators as part of their readership. This is important work, of course. But it begs the question: where is the content for male survivors? Male survivors vastly outnumber male perpetrators (ONS, 2023), but there are few tips on sex, communication, fertility or love aimed at us. It says something chilling about male culture if we find it easier to share the pool of knowledge with sex offenders rather than victims.

And yet we know, don't we? We know this is a lie. We know that no one is really simple.

In my late teens, I had a lover who was on testosterone. I didn't ask too many questions at the time about how they described themselves. I'd like to say I was wary of exoticizing them, that I understood that trans bodies are often fetishized and I was being sensitive.

The truth is that I didn't ask because I didn't want to appear uncool.

As D's body changed, our sex changed from intense to exuberant over the course of a few months. They were trying out a new way of being; I recognized the cheekiness masking a hunger to touch, to be wanted, to be permitted access to someone else's skin. Our sex was fun, in a giddy, giggly kind of way.

I was lucky. D shared the fun parts of their transition with me, and we never had the kind of relationship where I had to support them properly. I don't know whether D was a survivor of sexual violence. At the time, I didn't think of myself as belonging to that category.

Transgender men face similar rates of abuse – around that 47 per cent figure – to cis bisexual men. We don't know why this number is so high; it is higher than the prevalence of sexual violence for both gay and straight cisgender men, and higher even than the rates of violence against cisgender lesbian and straight women. Only women who are either bisexual, transgender or both face higher rates of sexual abuse.

We also don't know whether this risk is heightened for men

who fall into both categories; evidence about both our communities is scarce thanks to a chronic lack of interest from academic institutions. Where bi and trans identity intersect, this lack of interest stacks upon itself. Where members of the non-binary community are concerned, our broader understanding might as well be a ship in the Bermuda Triangle.

D showed up one night. I pushed them gently against the wall and they reached up to turn the light off. It was different from usual. It was as if a dam had broken and we were pouring into each other.

And then they stopped. Froze.

"Are you alright?" I asked, pulling back.

"Can we not?" they said.

We curled up together in my bed and listened to the seagulls. We didn't talk. We didn't have sex. D's hand held mine, solidly and almost aggressively. I remember realizing I needed to pee and putting off the moment where I'd have to get up and leave them alone.

Around seven we wrapped up warm – I lent D a leather trenchcoat I've never been brave enough to wear – and we braved the seafront to see whether the pancake stand at the pier was open.

"Lemon and sugar supremacy," D said. I disagreed for the sake of it and argued for Nutella.

"Porque no los dos?" they laughed.

We held hands on the walk down, D's fingers threaded through mine. I'd never held hands with someone in public before. In my relationship with Oliver we'd both been wary of the highwire, the dangerous feeling of being so publicly queer. Even in my next relationship with a woman, I hadn't been able to shake the feeling of fear that came with holding hands in public.

It was my last first. I'd had relationships, fucked, been to orgies. I'd cared for partners after surgery and had my heart broken. But I'd never held hands in public before.

The pancake place was closed, so we walked and walked and walked. I started imagining what it might be like to be together properly. To go for walks along the seafront and buy pancakes, and walk home with sugar on our lips.

"So, I'm moving to Melbourne in a few months," D said.

"Oh." My stomach moved towards my ankles. "Oh, cool."

"I think I have a real shot there," they said. Light filtered slowly through the clouds; the darkness thinning out and receding. I squeezed D's hand and smiled. I wished them well.

"I'll miss you though," they said. "You're cool."

We turned back in the hope of getting pancakes, hand in hand.

Why am I telling you this? Partly because I think it is important to illustrate the connections between bi+ men, trans men and trans mascs. Even when we hold only one of those identities, we still find ourselves trotted out as theoreticals. We exist rhetorically in arguments or as curiosities, but that's pretty much it. Partly I am telling you because I want you to believe that bi+ men are capable of gentleness and honesty and tenderness, and because I have come across so many people who are surprised by that fact.

But mostly I am telling you this because, in the face of academic and social indifference, this is still the only place where I can go to understand how a bisexual man who has experienced sexual violence navigates the world. We exist, bodies of knowledge without a home, briefly touching, sharing, inventing and reinventing masculinity. And I believe that many of the ways we do so could be of real benefit to the rest of the LGBTQ community and society as a whole.

But we won't know until we take the time to ask.

References

Brown, B. (2011). "The Power of Vulnerability" [video]. *TED Conferences*. https://www.youtube.com/watch?v=iCvmsMzlF7o [accessed 15 January 2024].

Brown, B. (2013). *Men, Women and Worthiness*. Audible. www.audible.co.uk/pd/Men-Women-and-Worthiness-Audiobook/B00C9IW0VI.

Browning, B. (2021). "Bi man ordered to pay ex-wife 'emotional damages' for coming out...but that got overturned." LGBTQ Nation, 3 August 2021. www.lgbtqnation.com/2021/08/bi-man-ordered-pay-ex-wife-emotional-damages-coming-got-overturned.

Frieden, Thomas R., et al. (2012) *The National Intimate Partner and Sexual Violence Survey 2010 Findings on Victimization by Sexual Orientation National Center for Injury Prevention and Control Division of Violence Prevention*. National Center for Injury Prevention and Control. www.cdc.gov/violenceprevention/pdf/nisvs_sofindings.pdf.

Jabbour, J., Holmes, L., Sylva, D., Hsu, K.J. *et al.* (2020). Robust evidence for bisexual orientation among men. *Proceedings of the National Academy of Sciences*, 117(31), 18369–18377.

Office for National Statistics (ONS), released 23 March 2023, *ONS website, statistical bulletin: Sexual offences in England and Wales overview: year ending March 2022*. https://www.ons.gov.uk/peoplepopulationandcommunity/crimeandjustice/bulletins/sexualoffencesinenglandandwalesoverview/march2022.

Pallotta-Chiarolli, M. (2015). *Women in Relationships with Bisexual Men: Bi Men By Women*. New York, NY: Lexington Books.

CHAPTER 4

Dual(ing) Identities

Being Working Class in the British Bi+ Community

Libby Baxter-Williams

Libby Baxter-Williams (she/her) has been involved in bi+ organizing and advocacy since 2006 when she attended her first BiCon. She is Director of Biscuit, the organization for bi+ people living in the UK, and she lives in South London with far too many shoes.

Bi+ people are, in the LGBTQ community, an often overlooked majority, just like working-class people in the UK. There are commonalities to our struggles, and not just in the way we are invisibilized as a community and forcibly positioned as outsiders. Our solidarity should be baked in.

But it is not. Working-class people are underrepresented in the bi+ community, and those who break through the barriers to inclusion are faced with prejudice and misunderstanding.

Class incontrovertibly matters in the UK. We can't really agree on what the classes are – are there three, as in the traditional model? Or are there seven, less distinct, classes? Are they defined by tax bracket? Cultural capital? Or is it more complicated than that? Certainly, we all experience class differently. It is imposed on us as a set of stereotypes and expectations, and our experiences are influenced by factors as significant as hometown and schooling and as seemingly minor as food choices. We *feel* our class. It simply is. We know it in ourselves and we intuit it in others. It informs our careers and our relationships, our family ambitions and our social circles. It seeps into every corner of our existence, pushing us forward, holding us back.

Many identify with the traditional model of stratifying class; UK government figures show that 48 per cent of people in the UK identify themselves as working class, a further 36 per cent or so as middle class. Only 11 per cent said none of these (Social Mobility Commission, 2021). The definition and taxonomy of the bi+ community (should such a monolith exist) is just as muddy as that of class. Nevertheless, the census shows bi+ people make up a little under half of the British LGBTQ community (Barton, 2023). It seems fair then to extrapolate that working-class bisexuals are not rare, but hidden.

Bisexual people are less likely, according to Stonewall and YouGov figures released in 2020, to be out than gay men and lesbians, with just 20 per cent of bisexuals open about their sexuality to their family and 35 per cent to their friends (Melville & Stonborough, 2020). The same survey data reveals that 42 per cent of bi+ people have actively hidden their orientation at work for fear of discrimination. These surveys do not address class directly, but data from the Office for National Statistics in 2013 revealed that those in middle-class work roles were 60 per cent more likely to describe themselves as gay, lesbian or bisexual (Bingham, 2014). Taken together these figures strongly suggest that outness is a privilege not afforded to all, and working-class bi+ people are among the least visible.

Despite their majority, working-class people do not control the cultural narrative in mainstream society, and bi+ people do not control the cultural narrative in queer communities. Instead, both are pressured to assimilate through upward mobility or "picking a side". To be working class and bi+, then, is to exist in the eyes of others in a state of unfulfilled potential on two fronts. We are assumed to be unsatisfied with our status, urged to adopt the supposedly superior values of the middle-class and monosexual (homo- or heterosexual) mainstream, and presumed to desire this. It is considered anathema that we might be happy where we are.

I am not a theorist, I'm an organizer. What follows, then, is not a meticulously cited academic essay (though I will provide sources for any statistics provided), but the product of several conversations with bi- and pansexual working-class people as well as my own experiences. It will look at the images of working-class bi+ people we see in the media, before going on to address barriers to participation in the bi+ community for working-class individuals, and the prejudice we face when we get there, but it will not attempt to solve these issues. Nor will it address the specific but related issues of antiziganism and whorephobia in the bi+ community. These issues deserve attention which I lack the lived experience to provide.

Representation in popular culture

Much has been written about how bi+ people and identities are portrayed in broadcast media, and with good reason. According to the TV Licencing Authority, 92 per cent of UK households own at least one television (Laricchia, 2023), and this ubiquity means it is second only to the internet as a method of consuming cultural content.

Across genre and timeslot, bi+ sexualities are not entirely

uncommon on British TV. Captain Jack Harkness from the BBC's *Doctor Who* and *Torchwood*, an omnisexual, time-travelling conman from the 51st century, is arguably the most well-known example. *Doctor Who* also gives us the Doctor's wife River Song, Clara Oswald, companion to Matt Smith and Peter Capaldi's Doctors, and blink and you'll miss them characters such as the Roman soldier Lucius in the 2008 episode "The Fires of Pompeii".

In recent years, British primetime has given us notable bisexuals in the eponymous *Fleabag*, the protagonists of Mae Martin's *Feel Good* and Desiree Akhavan's *The Bisexual*, as well as *Killing Eve's* Villanelle. The teen comedy *Sex Education* has a wealth of bi- and pansexual characters. Whether or not these are good representations of bi+ sexualities is subjective, and outside the remit of this chapter. What is worth noting is that these characters are all portrayed as comfortably middle class. It is signalled through their accent and wardrobe, their finances and their friends. They are creatives and professionals (or offspring of the same) with few money worries and central London flats, who have time and energy to expend on complicated personal lives. Only the Sky One comedy-drama *Brassic* supplies an example of a working-class bisexual character. His name is Tommo and he is a loner and a free-spirit but a fiercely good friend. Working as a sex worker in his own dungeon that seems to skirt the fringes of legality, Tommo is depicted as intensely hypersexual in both his professional and private life. As our only representative in the genre, Tommo's stereotypicality when it comes to his non-conformist nature and non-mainstream sexual practices is balanced by his uncomplicated plain speaking and genuine warmth towards his loved ones.

I would be remiss not to mention the practical reasons for the dearth of working-class characters in primetime TV: worldly concerns get in the way of storytelling. People do not go to the toilet and they do not worry about paying their Council Tax. Middle-class concerns are considered universal in a way that working-class stories aren't and it is not entirely the fault of producers. We like characters who live lives we can aspire to: have-it-all mums; glamorous twentysomething daters and even sociopaths, if they've got nice enough kitchens. Television is, after all, a form of escapism, and we rarely want to see our favourite characters queuing at the Jobcentre, doing the washing up and taking out the seams of last year's school trousers.

In primetime TV, middle class may be the default when it comes to bisexuality but it is curious to note that in broadcast media aimed more directly at a working-class audience, bisexual characters are not scarce. British soap operas (watched by around a quarter of the population) in particular have embraced both behaviourally bisexual and self-identified bisexual characters. Yorkshire Dales-set soap *Emmerdale* has had three bisexual characters to date, in Charity Dingle, Ivan Jones and Robert Sugden. *EastEnders* has Ash Kaur, *Hollyoaks* has Grace Black and Peri Lomax and *Coronation Street* has Tracy Barlow and Amber Kalirai. Welsh-language soap opera *Pobol y Cwm* has Gwyneth Jones and Britt Monk. Bisexuality is clearly suited to the longest of long-form storytelling. With the potential to develop a character over years or even decades, there is room for expansive exploration.

Outside soaps, working-class bi+ characters are practically unknown. The 1999–2006 ITV prison drama *Bad Girls* gave us Shell Dockley, the manipulative, violent and cruel inmate, the centre of a bisexual love triangle. Shell embodies the depraved bisexual trope perfectly, hitting her marks in sexual manipulation, cold-blooded sociopathy and general villainy. In this she echoes Villanelle. *Shameless*, which ran on Channel Four from 2004 to 2013, and which follows the lives and loves of the working-class Gallagher family, also gives us a bisexual character in Monica, ex-wife to Frank and lover to Norma. She is immature and duplicitous, absent from the family home for long stretches. Like Shell, we are not supposed to like, identify with or aspire to be her.

In 2020, the BBCs own *Creative Diversity Report* admitted that "often those from lower socio-economic backgrounds are depicted negatively, fuelled by stereotypes and seen as the object of ridicule" and this is certainly the case when it comes to bi+ characters (Sarpong, 2020, p.15). Where we exist at all we are immoral or amoral, overtly sexual, manipulative and flighty. We do not have rich inner lives, and, as GLAADs *Where We Are On TV* 2022–2023 report (Deerwater & Townsend, 2023) confirms, this is reflected in imported US media too.

Middle-class viewers are simply not being shown authentic working-class stories. We use fiction (not just televised) to make sense of our worlds, so being invisible in broadcast media is close to being invisible in the culture as a whole, and if we want our communities to recognize our whole selves, more diversity in storytelling is a must.

Barriers to participation in the community

The UK does not like easy classification, especially when it comes to social class and wealth. As we have discussed, we intuit class from invisible cues. These are reinforced by representation, or lack of representation, in the media, and we don't all come to the same conclusions. We're apt to describe Premier League footballers as working class, and low-paid but salaried call centre workers as middle class instinctually, but then argue income or wealth as the primary indicator of social class despite this (Parker Humphreys, 2020). We know that cultural capital matters but we can't agree on how much, or where it comes from, or even what it is.

Defining one's class in terms of relationship to the means of production is no longer a particularly useful metric. Today, fewer than 30 per cent of working-class people work in "traditional" industrial occupations such as factory worker, cleaner or tradesperson, with insecure desk-based roles and the service and care industries now in the majority, creating a "precariat" that lives pay cheque to pay cheque (Savage, 2015). What we historically have termed the working class was redefined following the Great British Class Survey published in 2011 and undertaken by academic researchers (Jones, 2017). They suggest this precariat, as well as what they term "emergent service workers", are the bottom rungs of the British class structure alongside the traditional working class. Rising housing costs, stagnant wages and now the global Covid-19 pandemic, and the decade of austerity before that, have had a devastating effect on the personal finances of all these groups.

Researchers (Badgett, Choi & Wilson, 2019) at the Williams Institute in the USA in 2019 found that 30 per cent of bi+ women and 20 per cent of bi+ men live below the federally mandated poverty line, and there is no evidence to suggest bisexual communities in the UK fare better. In fact, in 2014, a University of Essex study (Uhrig, 2014) found that gay men and bisexual men and women in the UK are more likely to be on a low income than their heterosexual counterparts. We are not a wealthy community, and with this as the backdrop the gap between the haves and the have-nots is made stark.

The British bi+ community can, largely, be split into the activist arm and the social arm, with the former agitating for change and the latter building community spaces. Both, though, require significant disposable income to participate.

Social meet-ups are held in pubs and cafes. Dance parties, club nights and discos have a cover charge. Drinks are exchanged on a tit-for-tat basis – you buy these, I'll get the next round in. Even a picnic in the park requires a bus fare. Many of the social rituals that build our friendships and communities cost money, and when the budget is tight, "unnecessary" social expenses are the first to be dropped. For those living on state benefits – Job Seekers' Allowance is, for example, at the time of writing, £84.80 (or £67.20 for under 25s) a week, paid fortnightly – the situation is even more bleak. Utility payments, rent and servicing debt must come first. In 2019, the UK Government's Social Mobility Commission found that people from working-class backgrounds in professional roles earn 17 per cent less than their more privileged colleagues, suggesting that social mobility does not come with all the benefits it promises, and even those with higher incomes are not on a level playing field with their heterosexual colleagues.

With little financial input from charities, grant-giving foundations and trusts, the British bi+ community's activism, just as elsewhere in the Western world, is largely self-funded. Our reach is limited by our own shallow pockets. In the UK, bi+ activists from low-income households represent significant numbers in both organized and individual bi+-specific activism, with precarious income juggled to fund community events, outreach, literature and grassroots organizing. Mutual aid practices are widespread, though may not be referred to as such, with relatively small amounts of cash donated to crowd-funders or given directly to a person in need criss-crossing the community weekly. Attending meetings could mean arranging for childcare for a few hours, and spending the money on a bus fare to a meeting could mean skipping a meal. Our ability to manage a shoestring budget comes in handy in bi+ organizing.

Adding further to the financial barriers faced by the working-class members of the bi+ community, demographic surveys undertaken by BiCon (2021), the annual national event for bi+ people, strongly suggest that bi+ people are more likely than the general population to be living with a disability. This is supported by research undertaken by Disabled World (2022), which found that 36 per cent of bisexual women and 40 per cent of bisexual men were living with a disability. Ill-health is expensive, even in a country with socialized healthcare. Work opportunities are limited, transport often costs more. Physical and mental energy are drained faster. Minority stress exacerbates minority stress, growing exponentially.

Time is often short in working-class households, too. Long work shifts, child and elder care, and prison visits are not issues confined to working-class households, but they are certainly more likely to be present. Energy is a limited resource, and more lacking in households on low incomes. Mental energy is drained by stress and worry, concerns about paying the bills; caring responsibilities, interpersonal relationships and lack of social support are again not limited to working-class households but are exacerbated by the ever-present underlying anxiety of insecure living.

Activism and organizing at the level the bi+ community finds itself relies strongly on reputation and connections. You can write an email to a potential ally that might never be read, or never get past their assistant, but a personal introduction is priceless. When you find among your social circle more zero-hours contracts than bankers bonuses, those connections are scarce, and, when made, come with a set of unspoken expectations, professional and personal, that feed impostor syndrome and feelings of alienation, often succinctly expressed in the phrase "my face just didn't fit".

Working-class women, as in wider society, are expected to take on caregiving roles in the community, as nurturers of the community as a whole, and of the overlapping social groups, special interest groups, and individuals within it. Conditioned by society to nurture, women, and those perceived as women, are corralled into roles that deplete physical and mental energy. This is not to say such people resent their work. It is often undertaken gladly and willingly and is rewarding mentally too, but the labour of care is intense and draining.

All this supposes working-class bi+ people can access resources in the first place. Participation in bi+ communities relies on access to resources – money, time, energy – less available to working-class people, and it is no surprise that we are an underrepresented group.

Classism in bi+ communities

Despite what many middle-class-identified people told me while I was preparing to write this chapter, it is decidedly not my experience that prejudice against bi+ people and communities is more common among working-class people than our middle-class counterparts. Authenticity is, after all, a working-class value. We are nevertheless perceived by outsiders to be more rigid and small-minded in our thinking and more likely to hold traditionalist values. This does not mesh well with the bisexual stereotype of Bohemian free love, and thus the possibility of a working-class bi+ person is rarely considered. One of the most commonly and sincerely held negative assumptions about bisexual people – that we are greedy – is also difficult to map on to working-class communities. Greed invokes the traditionally upper middle-class attributes of overconsumption and excess, not the working-class value of restraint. The human psyche is hardwired to sort information and when we're faced with stark contradictions we resist. We prefer "or" to "and", discrete categories to constant flux.

We are a nation of lazy thinkers, and stereotypes abound. Working-class communities are considered both socially conservative and politically radical, often by the same people. We contort what we have perceived to suit our presupposed ideas, often sincerely believing contradictory statements to be equally valid (e.g. we believe working-class people to be salt-of-the-earth grafters but also workshy and idle), handily forgetting whichever stereotype does not support the argument we are trying to make.

Working class is considered in the common consciousness to be synonymous with white (indeed, Black and working-class communities are considered to be in opposition); working-class people are derided as feckless and irresponsible at best and criminal at worst, and this, again, is magnified if you happen also to be from a racialized minority. Working-class people are fetishized and hypersexualized, women more so, and Black women, women of colour, and Gypsy Roma Traveller women especially. These stereotypes do not stop at the door: class hierarchies and sensibilities are undeniably reproduced both in queer communities at large and bi+ communities specifically. The romanticization of poverty and struggle as righteous is as prevalent in queer communities as any, and this further complicates matters.

Stereotypes are not the only weight under which working-class bisexuals suffer. Microaggressions, those daily slights that are rooted in bias or prejudice, are pervasive and cumulative, and often unwitting. Comments about accent, jewellery choices, where you work, live and come from, assumptions about intelligence and cultural awareness, education and family background are as commonplace within bi+ communities as outside them.

Respectability politics, the belief that marginalized communities must reflect the cultural norms of the dominant group in order to be worthy of respect, find their place in bi+ and queer communities with the policing of language, identity and behaviour with the aim of projecting to the mainstream the image of the idealized bisexual, sexless and politically moderate, polite and discreet, sanitized and palatable to middle England. Bi+ people are shamed for conforming to stereotypes and for voicing their justified anger just as working-class people are. Both groups too are assumed to be politically radical by default and despite evidence of wide-ranging political views. This is an important commonality on which to build mutual understanding.

Social alienation, that feeling of disconnection from the ingroup, is widespread. Impostor syndrome gets to many of us, and manifests in the belief you are a fraud. Both as bi+ people in the queer community, and as working-class people in the social hierarchy, we notice where we don't quite slot into place, and wonder if others have noticed it too.

In my informal conversations with bi+ people while preparing for this chapter, two specific classist assumptions were repeatedly raised as being particularly ubiquitous in bi+ communities, namely the hypersexualization of bisexual working-class women, and what I term class denialism: the assumption that bi+ people are middle class by default.

The perceived sexual availability of bi+ women, both cis and trans, is certainly a contributing factor to bi+ people's alarming rates of rape and sexual assault – statistics from the USA in 2010

(National Intimate Partner and Sexual Violence Survey, 2010) revealed that 61 per cent of bi+ women and 37 per cent of bi+ men have been victims of a sexual crime. Bisexuality, with its inferred promiscuity, amplifies the supposed sexual availability of working-class people. The phenomenon of "chav parties" and "scally nights", recently rebranded as sportswear nights, where attendees caricature and fetishize the stereotypical uniform of "Benefits Britain", and which are mainly confined to male-dominated queer spaces, both exemplify and exacerbate this.

Class denialism is a curious phenomenon. It speaks to a fear of class mobility, for what goes up can certainly come down, and it speaks to comfort in the status quo. It comes in many forms, from outright statements that "you're not working class" to sly digs about academic achievement or university attendance, perceived upward mobility or even relationship style (e.g. polyamory is seen as a middle-class phenomenon). The insistence that the bi+ community is 100 per cent middle class instils a sense of security and fellowship in those who claim it, for it is easier to be one for all if all are the same. Class denialism is also a function of respectability politics – we are shamed for conforming to working-class stereotypes, but if we don't conform, if we have the slightest academic bent, if we temper regional accents, if we have a career rather than a job, if we "pass" as middle class as a defence mechanism, our identity is denied to us. Bi+ people know what it is to have your identity erased, to have your marginalized status questioned. Why do we do it to each other?

There are benefits to more diverse communities beyond the box-tickingly obvious. The diversity of our class origins has an inevitable effect on our politics, and not just our ideals, but our methods for making ourselves heard.

It is hard to write about class in British society and harder to talk about it in microcosm. It almost seems radical enough to assert that a bi+ working-class population exists, much less that they are a community, and a part of the wider one, ever circling outwards.

But exist one does.

Working-class bisexual+ people are socially alienated, unable to integrate into the in-group and thus made powerless, battling a confusing set of middle-class values, fetishized for our authenticity and belittled for our ignorance of middle-class social norms. We are made a community by our outsider status, linked by what we are not as much as what we are.

"There is a division that runs right through the heart of the gay community based on class. And this affects people's experience of oppression, their politics, and their strategy for fighting for liberation," said Peter Morgan in a 1998 issue of *International Socialism*, and the fact remains that to be both bi+ and working class in the UK is to be a part of two invisibilized majorities. United by a shared sexuality, we are divided by the invisible hierarchies which dictate our experiences of what it means to be a community, to be marginalized, to be individuals and to be a group. Working-class integration begins with accessibility, but where it ends could be anywhere.

References

Badgett, M.L., Choi, S.K. & Wilson, B.D.M. (2019). *LGBT Poverty in the United States: A Study of Differences between Sexual Orientation and Gender Identity Groups*. Los Angeles, CA: The Williams Institute.

Barton, C. (2023). "2021 Census: What Do We Know about the LGBT+ Population?" House of Commons Library, UK Parliament, 16 January 2023. https://commonslibrary.parliament.uk/2021-census-what-do-we-know-about-the-lgbt-population.

BiCon (2021). "Demographics Survey Results and Comments." https://2021.bicon.org.uk/post-bicon-info-and-reccs/demographics-survey-

results-and-comments/?fbclid=IwAR2oqFOw9cibpwlSIOyfKYABK_
RauSnSo7ngyU1cMxMrgH6Bj9v-XFqyucM.

Bingham, J. (2014). "Middle class Britons 60 per cent more likely to admit to being gay." *The Telegraph*, 14 October 2014. www.telegraph.co.uk/women/sex/11145935/Middle-class-Britons-60-per-cent-more-likely-to-admit-to-being-gay.html?onwardjourney=584162_v1.

Deerwater, R. & Townsend, M. (2023). *Where We Are on TV 2022–2023*. GLAAD. https://glaad.org/whereweareontv22.

Disabled World. (2022). LGBT and Disability: Information, News, Fact Sheets. www.disabled-world.com/disability/sexuality/lgbt.

Jones, S. (2017). "Great British Class Survey finds seven social classes in UK." *The Guardian*, 3 December 2017. www.theguardian.com/society/2013/apr/03/great-british-class-survey-seven.

Laricchia, F. (2023). "Household ownership of digital TV in the United Kingdom (UK) 2007–2021." Statista, www.statista.com/statistics/956238/ownership-of-digital-tv-uk.

Melville, S. & Stonborough, E. (2020). *LGBT in Britain: Bi Report*. Stonewall. www.stonewall.org.uk/system/files/lgbt_in_britain_bi.pdf.

Morgan, P. (1998). Class divisions in the gay community. *International Socialism*, March 1998. www.marxists.org/history/etol/newspape/isj2/1998/isj2-078/morgan.htm.

National Intimate Partner and Sexual Violence Survey (2010). *NISVS: An Overview of 2010 Findings on Victimization by Sexual Orientation* www.cdc.gov/violenceprevention/pdf/cdc_nisvs_victimization_final-a.pdf.

Parker Humphreys, J. (2020). "Matt Hancock thinks footballers should be paid less because they're working class." Novara Media, 10 April 2020. novaramedia.com/2020/04/10/matt-hancock-thinks-footballers-should-be-paid-less-because-theyre-working-class.

Sarpong, J. (2020). *Creative Diversity Report*. BBC. http://downloads.bbc.co.uk/aboutthebbc/reports/reports/creative-diversity-report-2020.pdf.

Savage, M. (2015). *Social Class in the 21st Century*. London: Pelican.

Social Mobility Commission. (2019). *Social Mobility in Great Britain – State of the Nation 2018 to 2019*. www.gov.uk/government/publications/social-mobility-in-great-britain-state-of-the-nation-2018-to-2019.

Social Mobility Commission. (2021). *Social Mobility Barometer – Public Attitudes to Social Mobility in the UK*. www.gov.uk/government/publications/social-mobility-barometer-2021/social-mobility-barometer-public-attitudes-to-social-mobility-in-the-uk.

Uhrig, S.C.N. (2014). *An Examination of Poverty and Sexual Orientation in the UK*. Institute for Social and Economic Research. www.iser.essex.ac.uk/wp-content/uploads/files/working-papers/iser/2014-02.pdf.

CHAPTER 5

Bi Muslims Exist

Hafsa Qureshi

Hafsa Qureshi (any pronouns) is an openly bi and genderqueer Muslim, working to raise visibility and awareness for their community. By talking about faith, sexuality and disability, Hafsa wants to help destigmatize people's perceptions of queer people of faith. They currently work within LGBTQ+ inclusion and are a trustee at Gendered Intelligence.

I'm a lot of adjectives: Muslim, bi, genderqueer, Indian, hijabi, autistic, disabled... My identity reads like a checklist for a diversity seminar. Put together, these words make a lot of people upset. All these aspects intersect to make me who I am, and how I move through the world. And it's been a process even accepting all of them. Being bi seems like such a small aspect of me compared to the others, and yet it's been the most divisive.

Being raised and socialized as female in South Asian culture can be exhausting – especially when you're queer. If you're a woman, you're expected to get a degree, to meet a man, get married, be an excellent daughter-in-law (unpaid housekeeper), and have many, many babies. Genderqueerness be damned. So, what happens if you're bi? Well, that's easy, you can still marry a man!

Being bi means you can choose, right? Your alarmed aunties are just grateful you're not "fully gay". Your bi identity is a shameful secret, but at least it can be "fixed".

Dating when you're bi, brown and Muslim can be a mine-field. Your dates assume you might be a virgin, or that you're asexual. And some of us are, but the immediate assumption can be pretty awkward. Worse still, is when your date thinks that you can't be a serious option. Because some of us brown bi Muslims aren't out to everyone. Or your date might assume that you secretly hate yourself and wish you could be straight and/or cis. You're just experimenting. Getting the bi out of your system before you settle down for real.

Being vaguely femme on the internet often means a lot of creepy messages. Being bi and Muslim means you get called "sister" before a random guy sends you a photo of his genitals. Very courteous. For some people, "bi" implies "will sleep with me *and* my wife". Any indication that you may or may not be a sexual person just fuels the flames. You exist solely as an additional "marital aid" to be used an anniversary gift. Bimisogyny is exhausting. I feel as if I need to hide so many parts of myself before I can be taken seriously. I am sex positive, I am poly-amorous, and yet I must project an image of constructed "purity" for the sake of our message as bi people of faith. With the moralization of sex and sex work, one cannot exist as vaguely femme and sex positive without consequence. Do I want my audience to listen when I say bi folk are suffering? Then I must follow the construct of what is now expected of us "appropriate" bis. We merely exist to dispel outdated stereotypes. We do not have multiple partners. We have never heard of sex. We would never engage in sex work, and we don't know what PrEP is.[1] To

---

1   PrEP is a drug taken by HIV-negative people to reduce the risk of getting HIV.

admit so is to admit that perhaps the stereotypes were true, therefore rolling back years and years of bi activism work.

Growing up as a Muslim woman, owning my own sexuality wasn't really an option. In my early years as a baby bi, flirting with anyone felt like breaking some unwritten rule. Add neurodivergence to the mix, and it's as if everyone is speaking a completely different language. It can be hard to disentangle yourself from who you've been raised to be. Even now, there are people who once knew me who are worried for my soul, concerned that I've gone down a dark path because of the very queer life I've chosen.

My identity is an aberration to some. I am extremely lucky to be financially independent. I can live exactly as I wish to, whether people think I'm damned or not. But that isn't the norm for other queer Muslims like me. I've heard and seen so many horror stories of people ostracized, kicked out, and much worse. What non-queer, non-Muslim people don't understand is why. It's not always about people's interpretations of religion. It's often to do with a deep-rooted belief that your life is over now. You're walking down a path they desperately want to save you from, and you won't even hear them. That is the kind interpretation. The less kind one is that you're being selfish by putting your own needs before others. But both viewpoints are still centring someone else, and giving them power over your own life.

As is the case for many South Asian people my age, my parents were immigrants. And living through the difficulties of a totally new way of life has its challenges. An adherence to traditionalism, so we don't lose our heritage in this Western country. A fervent belief that education, followed by marriage, can save anyone. Your family doesn't want you to struggle like they had to, so they do everything they can to protect you, not realizing that cocooning you from the real world will only make things more difficult.

I think back to when I was 18, ten years ago now. I'd agreed to see some rishtas, or marriage proposals, to appease concerned family friends. They were worried about my future, and who would provide for me. At no point was I given the agency of independence, not even in their thoughts. I had to get married, so a man could provide for me. And I sat there and allowed it, sitting across from a man who couldn't even make eye contact with me – not because he was religious, but because he had never socialized with women before. The first words he spoke were to ask his own mother to make him some tea. My auntie ushered me into another room to have me make it instead, because, "Beta [child], you have to learn these things if you want to get married."

It is so surreal looking back at that moment. I am married now, to a lovely poly queer who is also white and Catholic. I think that auntie would have a heart attack if they met them. Depending on our work schedules, I even make more money than my spouse sometimes! I live for the subversion of gender roles, after having to live by them for so long.

After feeling so confused about where I belonged, I found the queer community. And, even now, it's been...complicated. There are fellow queer people who always assume I'm straight, because of my religion. My hijab says so much for me, without me speaking. People would erase my bi identity based on assumptions about the person I was in a relationship with. And for all the positivity and representation around Pride, the mainstream world hasn't fully embraced people like me. We sit in a weird space. Queer Muslims are tolerated by some, hated by others and ignored by most.

I remember going to my first UK Black Pride event. It was so beautiful, being surrounded by other queer people of colour. I sat down on the grass in a little sunny patch. A white man came up to me from nowhere, shook my hand, and then started asking me about my identity. I've had this sort of thing happen a lot. Even the most well-meaning allies can make you feel ostracized when you're treated as an unusual creature. People have assumed I am homophobic, or asked what led me to being an ally. Even working for an LGBTQ+ charity, I am looked at with suspicion. I am given a look-over indiscreetly, before I'm always asked, "And you're...?" while someone waits for me to fill in the blanks. To explain why I'm here. Hell, why I'm queer, too.

I used to fill those blanks immediately, announcing my queerness at all times. Just to let people know that I was safe to be around, so that they would accept me. It took a friend asking me why I did that for me to snap out of it. If people assumed I was homophobic, that was their Islamophobia showing. If they can't fathom that people like me can be bi, that's their problem. I don't need to explain my existence to anyone. And perhaps that may seem selfish of me. But if you're happy, does it matter?

My South Asian community places immense pressure on individuals to put themselves aside. Happiness is a potential side effect, not a destination. The media loves to talk about forced marriages in South Asian communities, which are absolutely terrible. But much more common is an arranged marriage. Your parents meet your future spouse's parents, then you and your future spouse meet each other. Supervised, of course. Sometimes you even get what's called a "marriage passport" with some fun information about your potential life partner, such as what their job is, what their dad does for work, what their grandad does, their lineage, a little passport photo. You know, totally normal things.

Arranged marriages are so common, we even use the phrase "love marriage" to describe a marriage where the couple knew and loved each other before. Culturally, we often talk about getting married and then falling in love. Not the other way around. And likely not before you have children, because that's what everyone is expecting of you. I don't see this as some barbaric custom. Our families are trying to ensure the best future for us, the only way they know how. To some generations, the idea of being close to 30 with no kids, on purpose, is unfathomable.

People outside my culture can see it as totally backwards, unaware that there are people who purposefully seek out arranged marriages because that's what they want in life. As each new generation passes, this viewpoint is changing. Frankly, the economy can't support a single-income household any more. Both of you have to work to pay rent forever, because you'll never own a home. There is no "hard work" out of that one. But when we live through hard times, like so many are doing now, we come together as a community.

The mainstream queer community may reject me, other Muslims may reject me. But other queer Muslims always have my back. We all know what it's like, to grow up "wrong", to be a disappointment before you've even done anything of note in this world. Some of my queer Muslim friends are of faith, and others aren't. And as much as external media likes to portray ex-Muslims and Muslims as sworn enemies, we will always have a kinship. Regardless of what faith or spiritual belief we may have, many of us were raised in similar environments – a hot pressure cooker of needing to be academically brilliant, not too loud, and perfectly obedient. And we all rebelled. I love that for all of us.

Our rebellion led us to find other people just like us, and social media has been perfect for this. I never really thought social media of all things is what would bring so many of us together. Or even how it would affect my life so completely up until now.

In a way, I came out via social media. I was out at work when I was 21, but I didn't really talk to people outside work about it much. I wouldn't deny it, but no one ever asked. In less tolerant workplaces, I have been asked aggressively if I'm a lesbian or not. To which I've always sheepishly answered, no. I didn't add on, "I'm actually bi" to that no. I just wasn't quite ready yet.

The reason I came out at work in the first place is because the LGBTQ+ network directly asked if LGBTQ+ people of colour would like to get involved. I don't know what made me change my mind. It was also the first workplace where I declared myself bi on paper, because they were the first to ask in confidence. Other workplaces would carelessly leave diversity monitoring forms all over the place. A total GDPR (General Data Protection Regulation) nightmare. But the civil service, of all places, was the first place that really didn't care what my sexual orientation was.

I got very involved with the network and was eventually kindly nominated for a Stonewall Bi Role Model of the Year award. And I won. I'd never won anything before. When I found out I'd won, I called people and told them. That's how I fully came out as bi at 25 years old, almost four years ago. And ever since then, supporting my queer community has just felt completely right. That workplace wasn't perfect, and I still hold some bad memories of my time there, but it led to my path in bi activism, and I'll always be a little bit grateful for that.

Ever since that award, I've carried a bit of imposter syndrome with me. What gives me the right to tell people the hows and whys of being bi? But the more bi folk I meet, especially bi people of colour, the more I see how wrong I am. We have the authority to talk about ourselves. For too long, other people have put words in our mouths. Cis people have written at length about trans people, white authors about Black culture, and I'm sure the studies done by heterosexual people on us queers are numerous. We are experts on our own lived experience. I don't need a degree to speak about my life. I know what it feels like to live as a marginalized person. So do those who may be reading this now.

I don't come from privilege, but I live in a lovely queer bubble now. I am allowed to be completely out to everyone who knows me. I don't rely on others for food or shelter and that is a massive privilege. I am not at risk of harm, like so many of my bi Muslim siblings. Coming out is not as essential as the queer community makes it out to be. Sure, it changed my life path around a bit. But our safety is the most important thing. My heart goes out to my queer Muslim siblings who still have to sneak around and hide parts of themselves. It's survival, and also sometimes respect.

When your family has sacrificed everything for you, is it too much to ask? I think it is, but I am also in no position to judge someone else's choices. I wish non-Muslims understood this. There is so much pressure from the queer community to be out and proud, without stopping to think of how that isn't feasible for some of us. We are not ashamed of who we are, but sometimes, someone else pays the bills. I hope other people with the same privileges I have think about this more before they judge other closeted bi people.

We can use our privilege to provide a platform for more marginalized communities, to speak up ourselves and to recognize that not every bi person's story is the same. Some of us had it pretty easy, like me. Others are still waiting for the day they have enough saved up to leave home. It's tough to feel as if you're staying true to who you are, while also surviving as best you can. You may not know a ton of queer Muslims personally, but I can guarantee there are a lot more of us than you think! As we grow and I get to march side by side with my queer Muslim siblings at Pride, I'm grateful for all the wonderful people under our rainbow.

I sometimes think about how society has tried to erase us, and I remember Alfred Kinsey. He was a sexologist (it's a real thing, I swear!) active in his field in the late 1940s. According to data we have, Kinsey was bisexual and had an open marriage with his wife. As a young man, he tried to punish himself for his "homoerotic feelings", but as his interest in science grew, he became the "Father of the Sexual Revolution", studying and writing about sex and sexual attraction. He was a controversial man, but he wasn't going to let the straights do the talking for us. And even if we're imperfect in our words or practice, we can still learn. We can still educate. I'm not saying bi people started the revolution, but us bis do like to have everything, don't we?

CHAPTER 6

Bisexual Men? Existing? It's More Likely Than You Think

Vaneet Mehta

Vaneet Mehta (he/him) is an Indian bisexual man born and raised in Southall, West London. He is a software engineer, writer and public speaker and the founder of #BisexualMenExist, which went viral in 2020. He has appeared on numerous panels and delivered talks to various companies. He has written for Men's Health, Stonewall, GMFA, Metro UK, *OutLife and* Unicorn Magazine *and his work has been published in* The Bi-ble: New Testimonials, The Ampersand Project *and* The Sex Agenda. Bisexual Men Exist, *his first book, was released in 2023.*

Bisexual Men Exist. A simple statement, and yet so many people have a hard time believing it. Bisexual men are so readily erased, and so often sidelined. According to the masses, this statement just isn't true. Why?

The reasons for this are complex, so let's break it down. Monosexism is the structural and systemic idea that only monosexual identities (gay/lesbian and straight) are valid or legitimate forms of sexuality. Bisexuality, and all other identities, are subsequently erased. Not just on an individual level, but a structural one. Monosexism impacts representation, education, healthcare and so much more. But I'm getting ahead of myself.

Monosexism constructs a binary, as so often is the case in society, and people are categorized in one of two boxes (where one is often held in higher regard than the other). Which box someone is placed in, well that's another question.

Phallocentrism is the idea that your relationship, your attraction, your sexual experiences with "the penis" (not a singular penis, or your own penis, but "the penis", this mythical object that seems to hold so much power) define your sexuality. To be penetrated by a penis is to be altered, to be changed, permanently.

The most well-known example of this concept in action is the purity culture targeted at women. Women are often told to hold on to their virginity, that you only get one "first", that it's important. Analogies are often used to describe the freshness of their genitals. To have sex, to have their vagina penetrated by a penis, is to change them. For women who have sex with a lot of men, they are often branded as "sluts", and crude analogies are often used, usually involving a lock and some keys.

This treatment of women is bizarre and deeply misogynistic. You can clearly trace the origin of these claims back to phallocentrism. It is this same concept that is used to categorize bisexual people. Bisexual women tend to be seen as straight, while bisexual men tend to be seen as gay. Of course, bisexual non-binary people are doubly erased as gender presents as yet another binary – the entire idea of phallocentrism is incredibly cisnormative.

Bisexual men are then erased as gay men, as being penetrated by a penis is seen to alter or change us. Our sexuality is defined by this event and our masculinity is evaporated.

Both monosexism and phallocentrism are pervasive on a structural level and ultimately lead to the erasure of bisexual men. We are seen to not exist, we are confused or undecided, have yet to pick our true identity, or seen as actually gay, just closeted or on the "down low". These ideas boil down to the biphobia and bi-erasure that bisexual men experience day to day in their personal lives. Worse than this, these ideas become internalized and ingrained.

According to Stonewall (2018a), 46 per cent of bisexual men aren't out to anyone in their family, while only 14 per cent of them are out to everyone in their family. Compare this to gay men, where only 10 per cent of them aren't out to anyone in their family, while 59 per cent of them are out to everyone in their family, and an issue presents itself. Why is this the case?

Homophobia naturally impacts bisexual men. As a man, your attraction to men is seen as wrong, dirty, sinful. This will play a part in the reason why bisexual men don't come out, but not by itself. It can't be the full equation, otherwise, gay men would be similarly closeted. No, homophobia isn't working by itself, but in combination with monosexism and phallocentrism.

Sexuality is presented as a binary, and holding attraction for more than one gender at a time is seen as an impossibility. It is this notion that means that bisexual men often feel as if they have to make a choice, whether consciously or subconsciously, between gay and straight.

In this grossly homophobic society, bisexual men may identify as straight. This could be down to their inability to accept their attraction towards men, seeing it as wrong. Or they may feel the pressure to conform to expectations to identify as straight. They're still attracted to women, so why not just push down their attraction for men and other genders and lean into heteronormativity? It is the latter that often leads monosexual people to state that bisexual people have straight passing privilege, but this could not be further from the case (we'll get to this).

Conversely, due to phallocentrism, bisexual men may instead identify as gay. Society tells them they have to make a choice, gay or straight, and that their attraction to men (to "the penis") defines their identity. Therefore, they must be gay. Their attraction to women is most likely just the conditioning from a heteronormative society that tells them that men should be attracted to women. So they come out as gay, but their attraction to women and other genders never really disappears.

Coming out as bisexual is immensely difficult. Phallocentrism means they will never be seen as bisexual, but instead as closeted gay men. Dating a woman can be difficult as this view means the woman won't believe their attraction to them, and women are often concerned with the idea of the person leaving them for a man. Dating men isn't easier, as bisexual men are seen as closeted, as confused, and told to figure themselves out, to actually come out.

And when they do? They're seen as traitors, seen to be going back in the closet and abandoning the community. Because of course, bisexual people aren't part of it.

So coming out is difficult. There are barriers, both internal and external, which prevent bisexual men from opening up about their identity. They may struggle to accept their attraction to certain genders, or the fact that their attraction goes beyond a single gender. They may be acutely aware of how society sees multi-gender attraction, and fear how friends, family and loved ones may see them.

Dating as someone who is attracted to more than one gender may sound easier (all that choice!) but as we've seen, the structures at play make it so much harder to find people to date, as their preconceived notions of bisexuality often means they avoid us. Worse than this, our identity can lead to violence. Stonewall (2020) reported that 13 per cent of bi people had experienced unwanted sexual contact and 42 per cent of bi respondents felt their orientation may have been a motivating factor.

There are a multitude of ways this may have played out, all of which come back to the perceptions of bisexuality and multi-gendered attraction. Bisexual people are often seen as sexually promiscuous. Because we are attracted to more than one gender, we are seen as more sexually available – we're attracted to everyone. We are seen as greedy and insatiable because we are outside the norm of monosexual, of attraction to a single gender. This is clearly rooted in monosexism and it can lead to sexual violence, as our identity can lead people to believe that we are always "up for it", so to speak, that we want that sexual encounter even when we don't.

Violence can also be used as a means to convert or punish. A survey from Galop (2022) revealed that "20.5 per cent of poly-sexual respondents told us that they had experienced sexual violence which they believed was intended to convert or punish their LGBT+ identity" (p.3). For bisexual people, our identity isn't believed to exist and sexual violence may be used as a way to convert us to a monosexual identity, otherwise known as "corrective rape". If there is a biological reaction to stimulus (which is not uncommon during sexual assault) this may be read as arousal, which the assailant may use as "proof" that we are indeed attracted to them, and therefore indicating our "true" identity.

Is it any wonder that bisexual people stay closeted? That we may not tell people about the multitude of our attractions?

That we withhold our identity or identify in a different way altogether in order to escape harm or make certain aspects, like dating, easier?

Some believe that we have straight passing privilege as a result. If we can get into a "heterosexual" (or different gender) relationship and be happy in that relationship, then what is the problem? It sounds like a pretty easy life. You don't get slurs thrown at you on the street, you don't get attacked or abused in public. But it is missing the fact that even if you're happy, being closeted is still incredibly damaging to your mental health.

Stonewall (2018b) saw that bisexual men are more likely to have anxiety, more likely to self-harm and more likely to have suicidal ideation than gay men. Why? If straight passing privilege exists, why is there such a huge issue with mental health among bisexual men? The difficulties of coming out, of accepting your multi-gendered attraction, of dealing with biphobia and bi-erasure as people deny your identity, as they refuse to accept you...this all has an impact.

LGBTQIA+ people know that being closeted is damaging. This doesn't go away just because you're in a happy relationship. There is a constant fear of revealing your true identity, feeling the need to hide parts of yourself, to censor yourself. What if you let something slip? What if they find out? Even though your attraction for them remains the same, even if you want nothing about your relationship to change, coming out could still go terribly wrong.

What if they think you're actually gay? What if they think you're going to, or already have, cheated on them? What if they fear that you're eventually going to leave them for someone else, someone of a different gender? And what if, because of all of their thoughts and feelings on bisexuality, they leave you? It is easy to see how your mental health would be impacted by this.

Getting help for these issues isn't exactly easy. Long waiting lists make it hard to get help on the NHS and high costs of private care can be difficult to meet when bisexual people are more likely to live below the poverty level (Badgett, Durso & Schneebaum, 2013). But even after getting through this barrier and the barrier around mental health stigma, you may not receive the quality of care you would expect. As I have mentioned, monosexism is structural and pervasive. How can you get quality care if the person who is supposed to help you doesn't know anything about your identity or, worse, does not even believe it exists?

In 2020, a study was published in a psychological journal (Jabbour *et al.*, 2020) that proved the existence of bisexual men. Not satisfied with just asking, they decided to validate this existence by measuring men's penises to certain types of pornographic material to see their arousal. What does this say about the care that bisexual men may receive when trying to access therapy? If those in scientific fields can't believe bisexuality exists without "proof", will therapists be doubtful of their patient's identity?

Stonewall saw that bisexual men have to deal with probing questions and are made uncomfortable by healthcare professionals; 40 per cent of bisexual men also reported that they were not out to anyone when seeking medical care; 21 per cent of bi people said that healthcare professionals didn't understand their specific health needs; and 22 per cent of bi people experienced inappropriate curiosity from these professionals (Stonewall, 2020). You can see how monosexism causes structural issues; bisexual men are not able to get the care they need or deserve because those working in the field do not see bisexual as a legitimate sexuality. They do not understand their identity, let alone what they need. And the fear of bad encounters means bisexual people aren't disclosing their identity, which further prevents them from getting help.

Monosexism affects not only the mental health of bisexual men, but also their sexual health. During the AIDS crisis in the 1980s, bisexual men were villainized by mainstream media and painted as a vector for disease. These publications stated that bisexual men were the reason why HIV, largely seen as a "gay disease", was being passed to unsuspecting straight women and even their unborn babies. This gave rise to the "bisexual bridge theory", the idea that bisexual people bridge the gap between gay and straight communities.

Despite this, when Brian Dodge, a professor and researcher in the field of sexual health, came along in the early 2000s to try and conduct a pilot study to explore the issues bisexual men face in regard to HIV risk, he was met with constant obstacles (Dodge, 2015). Why? Because people didn't believe bisexual men existed. In fact, one grant reviewer demanded evidence that they existed and after Dodge provided some, the reviewer said the evidence was insufficient. Dodge was unable to get his research off the ground until he changed his terminology, using MSMW (men who have sex with men and women) instead. In his next meeting, it seemed as if his peers were more concerned about the risk they pose to their female partners.

Monosexism is a structural issue. The impact is beyond an interpersonal level, beyond getting erased by a friend or receiving biphobia on the street. Monosexism, in this case, is the main barrier that Dodge had to overcome in order to conduct his incredibly important research. If those in positions of power do not believe that bisexuality is a legitimate identity, if they believe there is not enough proof that bisexual men exist, then we can't even research the issues bisexual men are dealing with. Unfortunately, when you are able to convince those in charge that bisexual men do exist, they seem more concerned with the risk we pose, rather than the issues we face. Our care is not considered because we aren't seen as important.

This carries over even into the LGBTQIA+ community. In the 1980s, the London Lesbian & Gay Centre banned bisexual groups from their space. It was said that bisexual men were likely to harass lesbians, so were not allowed in the space. I can't say this would never happen; bisexual men are just as capable of being predatory as any other man, but to paint an entire community with the same brush and exclude them from a space is not okay. What about the needs of bisexual men to have a space? Why is this not a concern?

Well, despite the fact that bisexual people had been at the forefront of LGBTQIA+ rights movements (the mother of Pride is a bisexual woman named Brenda Howard), and despite the fact that bisexual people had been part of the community for years under the "lesbian and gay" banner, bisexuals were banned because they weren't lesbian or gay. So the space wasn't for us. This is why the needs of bisexual men, and bisexual people in general, aren't a concern.

To make matters worse, as more information came out during this time, it was mentioned that these bi groups had people who were heterosexual, the space was to be free of pressure from heterosexual society and these groups would be allowed in the space if they changed their name to include gay/lesbian in it. When you put all the pieces together, it seems as if the real issue was that the London Lesbian & Gay Centre did not see bisexuality as real. They saw bi people as straight people who are encroaching on and tainting their space.

The needs of bisexual men, their desire for a space, this isn't important because, again, we don't exist, and since we don't exist, why would we be considered?

The exclusion of bisexual people from LGBTQIA+ spaces hasn't gone away. Even in 2017, Pride in London nearly went ahead without a single bi group. When they were questioned on this, they said no one applied. But did anyone bother to reach out to bi groups to find out why? Seems unlikely, especially considering the fact that when they were called out by the bi community, they labelled bisexual activists as "demanding" (Shearing, 2018). Bisexual people often have to deal with discrimination not just from wider society but even within the LGBTQIA+ community, a concept known as double discrimination. Stonewall (2018a) saw that 18 per cent of bisexual men experienced discrimination in their local LGBTQIA+ community space, compared to only 4 per cent of gay men. This is likely the reason why 50 per cent of bisexual men do not attend their local spaces.

All of this creates a new barrier. For most LGBTQIA+ people, coming out can be a fraught process. You may lose friends or family, you could get thrown out of your home or cut off financially, you could be put in some dangerous situations. The saving grace, for those who have access to it, is often a local LGBTQIA+ space – a community centre, a cafe, a bar or club, a local group. Whatever form it takes, it can be a place to find friends, gain support, find information and resources, get help, build a network, and so much more.

But what do you do when those spaces aren't safe for you? If those spaces are rife with the same discrimination you experience on the outside? People telling you that you don't exist, saying you're confused or encouraging you to "come out all the way". Then what? All of that, the friends, the resources, the information and help, all become completely unavailable to you. The space isn't built with you in mind, so why bother going there?

This creates the cycle of invisibility. Bisexual men aren't in LGBTQIA+ spaces due to the discrimination they face or the general feeling that they just don't belong, that the community isn't made for them. When people are conducting research, surveys, studies on the community, they're likely going to LGBTQIA+ spaces, where bisexual men aren't present. They may be asking the wrong questions, such as focusing on whether bisexual men exist or the harm they cause to others, instead of what issues they face. They may not even ask any questions pertaining to bisexuality, since they don't even believe it exists.

This means that the issues that bisexual men face are never truly captured, their lived experiences never fully understood. So, of course, if you don't know what bisexual men are experiencing, then you can't ask what can be done to fix their issues. This means that no changes are made in order to better accommodate bisexual men. Spaces won't change their rules to make sure biphobia isn't tolerated, staff aren't trained to understand and assist bisexual men better and no new networks or groups are created specifically catering towards bisexual men. The exclusion is re-embedded into the system and continues to perpetuate itself as the cycle keeps on turning.

You can see how pervasive monosexism and phallocentrism are. They create barriers in so many different areas, which itself creates more barriers. Representation on screens is so often used to present sexuality as a binary, and even now as that is changing, bisexuality is often left unnamed, which leads viewers to place characters into the binary. Education in schools has been improving, at least in the UK, but can we trust them to do right by bisexuality when it still seems so elusive?

Researchers continue to ask the same old questions like "do bisexual people exist?" instead of focusing on the dire state of our health and well-being, and even our healthcare professionals aren't sure what to do with us. And the LGBTQIA+ community? Even they're doubtful of our existence, convinced we're actually closeted or encroaching on their space. They think we have it easier, that being bisexual is the easy way out. So are their networks, information, educational resources and spaces made for us? Unlikely.

How do you come out in an environment like this? How do you date with all these preconceived notions? How can you be proud of your identity when it doesn't even exist? It is impossible for so many – so many don't come out, don't go into spaces, hide their identity from friends, family, partners, even doctors. That lack of visibility only begets further invisibility. We aren't seen, so our issues, our struggles aren't seen. No one fixes...well, anything. Which makes the environment worse, which makes it even harder to come out.

Bisexual Men Exist. Such a simple statement. It seems so obvious. Yet it isn't. In 2019, I created the hashtag #Bisexual-MenExist. This trended worldwide in 2020. I started writing a book all about the topic and it was published in 2023. It's called *Bisexual Men Exist*. You may think it's obvious. You may wonder why it even needs to be said. You may find it ridiculous that someone can write over 200 pages on something that could be summed up in three, simple words. One obvious little phrase.

But exist it does, just like the bisexual men. It exists because there is not a single facet of society that seems to know it, and the harm that bisexual men have to deal with every day because of that is endless. This isn't just about being visible, even if the hashtag was just swathes of selfies (which is exactly what I asked for). It's not just about repeating these three words like a mantra to every person you meet. It's not just about having some more bi characters on TV.

It's about change: actual, real, structural change. Dismantling the structures that create this harm. It's about educating people on the spectrum of sexuality and how we shed these structures, these ways of thinking. It's about making space, uplifting and giving a platform to the voices of bisexual people. It's about funding bisexual organizations, which is so rarely done (Andre, 2012), so they can actually help their community.

This won't just make the lives of bisexual men better, but society as a whole. We saw early on how the concept of monosexism also harms bisexual women, how binary ideas in society are not limited to sexuality but impact gender too, and how phallocentrism harms all women. Bisexual men, in their fight against these harmful structures that negatively impact their lives, also hold the tools to fight oppressive structures that reach far beyond them. In their fight to improve society for themselves, they can also ally themselves with other marginalized folks and unite against these systems.

Bisexual Men Exist. If you didn't know before, you do now. And that's just the beginning. So...shall we begin?

References

Andre, A. (2012). "Show us the money: Funding for bisexual community lacking." Huffpost, 4 January 2012. www.huffpost.com/entry/bisexual-funding_b_1178932.

Badgett, M.V.L., Durso, L.E. & Schneebaum, A. (2013). New Patterns of Poverty in the Lesbian, Gay, and Bisexual Community Williams Institute. https://williamsinstitute.law.ucla.edu/wp-content/uploads/Poverty-LGB-Jun-2013.pdf.

Dodge, B. (2015). "Scientific Research on Bisexual Men: What Do We Know, and Why Don't We Know More?" In R. Ochs & H. Sharif Williams (eds), Rec.og.nize: The Voices of Bisexual Men 119-125. Boston, MA: Bisexual Resource Center.

Galop. (2022). The Use of Sexual Violence as an Attempt to Convert or Punish LGBT+ People in the UK. https://galop.org.uk/wp-content/

uploads/2022/01/The-Use-of-Sexual-Violence-as-an-Attempt-to-Convert-or-Punish-LGBT-People-in-the-UK.pdf.

Jabbour, J., Holmes, L., Sylva, D., Hsu, K.J. et al. (2020). Robust evidence for bisexual orientation among men. *Proceedings of the National Academy of Sciences*, 117(3), 18369–18377.

Shearing, L. (2018). "Why London Pride's first bi float was so important." The Queerness. https://thequeerness.com/2018/08/01/why-london-prides-first-bi-float-was-so-important.

Stonewall. (2018a). *LGBT in Britain: Home and Communities*. www.stonewall.org.uk/sites/default/files/lgbt_in_britain_home_and_communities.pdf.

Stonewall. (2018b). *LGBT in Britain: Health Report*. www.stonewall.org.uk/system/files/lgbt_in_britain_health.pdf.

Stonewall. (2020). *LGBT in Britain: Bi Report*. www.stonewall.org.uk/system/files/lgbt_in_britain_bi.pdf.

CHAPTER 7

I Couldn't Be Bisexual Without Polyamory

Zachary Zane

Zachary Zane (he/him) is the author of Boyslut: A Memoir and Manifesto *and co-author of* Men's Health Best. Sex. Ever. *He writes "Sexplain It", the sex and relationship advice column at Men's Health, and "Navigating Non-Monogamy", the polyamorous relationship column at Cosmopolitan. He is editor-in-chief of the BOYSLUT Zine, which publishes non-fiction erotica from kinksters across the globe. His work has been featured in the New York Times, Rolling Stone, Washington Post, Playboy, and more.*

Polyamory was never an option for me. Like nearly every single person across the globe, I was brought up with the notion that you had to settle down with one person. Then you had to pump out some rugrats and start a family. I didn't even know the word "polyamory" existed until college. When I first learned about the label, I didn't initially have disdain for it, the way many monogamous folks do. I wasn't one of those mono people who said, "Polyamory never works out long-term," or, "Isn't that the same as just 'dating around'? Why do you have to label it?" I didn't think their relationships were invalid or that monogamy was morally superior.

However, I did think it sounded a little hippy-dippy. My only comparison was the free love movement in the 1960s and 70s. So whenever I heard the term "polyamory", I imagined a sort of Kumbaya-style commune with people my parents' age on acid, wearing long, flowy gowns with sunflowers in their ears. That didn't appeal to me in the slightest. But all of this implies that I gave the relationship structure more than a few fleeting thoughts, which I did not. Polyamory did not take up any space in my mind until I came out as bisexual.

Like polyamory, bisexuality, initially, wasn't an option. And whereas I at least knew polyamory was "real", meaning that some people lived polyamorous lifestyles, I didn't think male bisexuality was real. Not until my second session of seeing a new LGBTQ-affirming therapist, who interrupted my rant about being sexually confused to say, "Correct me if I'm wrong, but it doesn't sound as if you're confused. It sounds as if you're clearly bisexual." I was quick to reply, "That shit doesn't exist in men," to which he responded, "Zach, you're too smart to think that."

He was the first health professional – the first person – to tell me that bisexuality exists in men. And, as he so eloquently stated, I am *clearly* bisexual. That conversation was a turning point for me. Soon after, I started to embrace being bisexual. Well, first I identified as bi-sexual – notice the hyphen – and heteroromantic, meaning that I was sexually attracted to all genders but only emotionally attracted to (and could date) women.

While a valid orientation, it simply wasn't mine. I only identified as such because I was still struggling with internalized biphobia. However, after a few months and a whirlwind night of passion with a man, I realized that I could indeed love a man. I was bisexual, biromantic, bi-everything.

Everything changed when I became bisexual, or rather, embraced my bisexuality. It changed how I viewed myself and the world. It helped me realize that there were other options in all aspects of my life, like there were more options than just being gay or straight. For example, the things I thought I "had" to do to be a successful person in this capitalistic hellhole were bullshit. I could forge my own path to success, make my own hours, and thrive! I also realized that I could forge my own path to relational success. Being bi opened up the idea that there was more than one way to think about partnerships and love. There are more options than being monogamous.

Still, I didn't immediately jump into polyamory the moment I proudly claimed the bi label. First off, I was still on the hunt for "the one". Second, I struggled immensely with jealousy. I would quickly grow insecure when my girlfriend was hit on by attractive men when we were out. I wasn't an asshole to my girlfriend about it. I never blamed or yelled at her. Instead, I became uncomfortable, mopey and clingy. Clearly, I wasn't cut out for polyamory. Or at least that's what I thought.

But at 23 years old, when my girlfriend and I broke up, I went into slut mode. We had been monogamous for almost a year and I desperately craved some hairy booty. So I went hard on Grindr – and that is saying something. I had a new boy over every day, often two. And you know what? I was happy. There's this misconception that if you're having sex with a lot of people, it means you're secretly miserable, seeking validation through sex, or using it as a distraction from larger issues. While this could be the case, let's not forget that sex is fun. It feels good! It's a great way to make new friends. Don't be an asshole and shame slutty people who are using sex for the sole purpose of fucking being an enjoyable partnered activity.

While I was in slut mode, there were two guys who I wanted to plow more than once. And they couldn't get enough of my dick either. I made it very clear to both of them that I was not looking for a committed relationship. Monogamy and being "boyfriends" were off the table.

A few months into our friends-with-benefits set-up, one of them asked me to be their monogamous boyfriend. I told him that wasn't something I could offer, and he was very upset with me. A few weeks later, I had the same conversation with the other man, and he cried profusely when I gave the same response.

I felt bad for these men. I really did like them, and in another world, we could have had a committed relationship. (Alas, we don't live on Earth-II, so it had to end.) But I also was frustrated. I made my expectations and what I could offer romantically crystal clear from the get-go. Then, when they asked for more, I was suddenly the "bad guy" when I said no. Both told me that I led them on. Untrue, I did the opposite!

So I made a rule: no more dates – just sex! Even a Netflix and Chill was too much. You had to be in and out of my apartment within 30 minutes. But then I met Jason, and let me tell you, I was not expecting to fall in love with someone like him! I met him at an underground fetish party in Boston. He was there with his boyfriend and informed me that he lived with his wife and girlfriend. I had to pick my jaw up off the floor. I was fascinated by their relationship structure, so I asked if I could interview him for an article. At the time, there wasn't nearly as much content about polyamory (and consensual non-monogamy) as there is now. This encounter took place in 2016, right before the vast influx of consensual non-monogamy content made its way to mainstream outlets.

So, we set a date for me to come over for "game night" to meet his wife, his wife's boyfriend, and their shared girlfriend. I had no idea what to expect. Foolishly, I thought there was the possibility for an orgy, so I douched, just in case. (Not all bi/poly people are slutty and immediately want to jump into bed with strangers they've just met. That's just me!) When I arrived, Jason's wife greeted me with a toothy smile and warm hug. I then met the rest of his polycule, who were all equally delighted to meet me. We had some wine and played games all night. (One of the most poly things to do!) If memory serves me correct, we played Dominion, which, aside, is one of the best strategic card games out there.

While warmth and love flowed from every corner of the house, something felt off. It almost felt "forced", for lack of a better word. It seemed as if every time one partner got a kiss, every other partner had to get a kiss, too. If one partner got a compliment, you had to compliment the other. I felt as if everyone was acting in a very calculated way so as not to show favouritism, and everyone had to be on "equal footing" at all times. It seemed not only exhausting but also impossible to sustain long term. Of course, at times, you'll feel closer with one partner, the way I sometimes feel closer with one of my brothers. (Still, that doesn't mean you love one partner more than the other!)

I felt that I was only seeing the very appealing facade of being polyamorous. I wasn't privy to what was happening behind the scenes – the jealousy, difficult conversations, and work.

So I figured polyamory wasn't for me, but since I enjoyed seeing them, I accepted every invitation for group hang-outs. Then, at one of these get-togethers, Jason surprised me by asking me out on a date. Even though I wasn't "dating", I agreed because I figured there was no way things could get serious. The man had a boyfriend, a girlfriend, a wife, and multiple other casual partners. He didn't have time to breathe, let alone have another committed relationship.

Well, I was wrong. One date led to two and two to five more. Before I knew it, I was seeing him almost every night. In hindsight, I have no idea how he made the time for me, but he did.

And just like that, I had a boyfriend. Four months later, in a turn of events no one could have predicted, I was living with him and his wife. (His wife's girlfriend and boyfriend were frequent houseguests who would stay for days, sometimes weeks on end.)

It was one of the best seven months of my life. In part, because I loved him dearly and partly because I was in a polyamorous relationship. This new relationship dynamic led to the healthiest and most fulfilling relationship I'd ever been in. I felt liberated both romantically and sexually.

Being able to step off the relationship escalator allowed me to be more present in the moment. For those unfamiliar with the term, the relationship escalator refers to the expected progression of a relationship. First, you meet on an app or through a friend and have a date. If the date goes well, you go on a couple more, and on the third date, you have sex. After four months, you decide to be monogamous and declare your partner your "boyfriend" or your "girlfriend". After six months, you say I love you. Eighteen months in, you get engaged, then married six months later, and lastly, you have a few kids and raise them.

To me, this sounds like a fate worse than hell. I hate having my life planned out without the ability to change. I'm not the man I was five years ago, five weeks ago, or even five days ago. I'm constantly growing, and I need for my relationship to have the ability to grow with me.

Poly people do not step on that relationship escalator. Instead, they blow that escalator to smithereens. They create their own type of relationship without these societal expectations. As a result, they don't define success by forever. Poly people understand that you can have a beautiful relationship that lasts six years or six months – just because you broke up, doesn't mean you "failed". It simply means you two had a beautiful relationship and were smart enough to end it when you did. You didn't feel compelled to keep it going, the way many monogamous folks do.

Having this mentality as a polyamorous person helped me to stop worrying all the damn time! I wasn't concerned with "where this was going" or anxious thinking about what the future may hold, like I had been in my monogamous relationships. I was able to enjoy my time with Jason in the now.

I also felt less pressure to be Jason's "everything". (He had a wife and multiple other partners to step in and support his various needs.) In my past monogamous relationships, it seemed as if I was responsible for my partner's happiness and wellbeing. We had nothing going on outside each other, so there was an unhealthy level of co-dependency. That added a lot of pressure to the relationship, and do you know what's not good for a relationship? Pressure! With Jason, we had a community of polyamorous friends and lovers who supported one another. Everything didn't fall on me.

Now for what it's worth, these reasons for preferring polyamory have nothing to do with being bisexual. They pertain to any sexual orientation. However, certain things I loved about polyamory were directly related to my (bi)sexuality.

First and foremost, I never felt I was "picking a side" when I was polyamorous. Previously, when I dated men, my lifestyle and friend group became very gay. When I dated a woman, we frequented straight bars, had more straight friends, and so on. But when I discovered polyamory, I was privy to both the straight and gay worlds. I could go to the Eagle with my boyfriend and get pounded by some hunky dudes one night, and the next night go to a Yankees game with my female partner.

Polyamory also introduced me to a new world – the "queer world". I didn't know that there was a community of bi, fluid, trans, and non-binary people who lived outside heteronormativity. These people don't float between the "gay" and "straight" worlds. They don't feel compelled to fit into any box. They have their own spaces and friends. They have their own ways they love and they don't conform to any heteronormative or homonormative ideals for a relationship. These are the people I hang out with the most. They are my friends, lovers and partners. (Often, they are all three!) They're the ones who make me feel loved, supported and extremely bisexual.

Second, it was affirming to be "visibly" bisexual. When I was monogamous and had a boyfriend, people assumed I was gay. When I had a girlfriend, people assumed I was straight (or was closeted and in denial about being gay). When I dated someone non-binary, I don't think people knew what to think. But when I said I have a boyfriend, a girlfriend, and a non-binary partner there's no fucking denying it: I'm bisexual. And while you don't need strangers to affirm your sexuality – you have friends and family to do that – it is still nice that people believe I am truly bisexual because it is exhausting justifying my sexuality all the time.

Third – and I know I spoke about this a little bit, but I want to make this point crystal clear – I met a HUGE bisexual community the moment I became poly, which aligns with research about bi people being significantly more likely to be poly than gay/straight folks. In her 2019 paper published in the *Journal of Sex Research*, Dr Rhonda Balzarini and her colleagues at the University of Western Ontario analysed the demographic backgrounds of 2428 polyamorous individuals and 539 monogamous folks by asking participants to take an online survey. Among other findings, Balzarini found that polyamorous people tend to identify more as bisexual/pansexual than any other sexual orientation.

I had always struggled to find bi friends and partners. Suddenly, when I became poly, all I knew were bi folks. It was fucking amazing to be surrounded by other bi people who understood and embraced my sexual identity.

Last but certainly not least, the sex! I didn't want to mention sex first because often, monogamous people think that being poly is *all* about sex. No, it's not all about sex, but I would be lying if I said it wasn't partially about sex.

Most bi people don't need to be sleeping with multiple genders in order to feel sexually satisfied. However, I am not most bi people! I am a slutty, greedy, bisexual stereotype who loves having sex with everyone of all genders and wouldn't want it any other way.

Polyamory has allowed me to have multiple sexual and romantic relationships with people of all genders simultaneously, and that is something I don't just want as a bisexual, it's something I need.

That's why I've come to realize that polyamory isn't just a lifestyle for me. It's part of my identity, just like bisexuality. The two are inextricably connected, and frankly, I wouldn't be able to live happily and fulfilled as a bisexual person, if I wasn't also polyamorous.

Reference

Balzarini, R., Dharma, C., Kohut, T., Holmes, B.M. *et al.* (2019). Demographic comparison of American individuals in polyamorous and monogamous relationships. *Journal of Sex Research*, 56(6), 681–694.

CHAPTER 8

Bisexuality and the Threat to TERF and Gender Critical Politics

Lois Shearing

Lois Shearing (they/she/he), known as Lumpi to their friends, is a bisexual and gender-fluid journalist, author and activist. Their first book, Bi the Way: The Bisexual Guide to Life, *was published by Jessica Kingsley Publishers in 2021. They're also the founder of the Bi Survivors Network, which supports bi, pan, and multi-gender-attracted survivors of sexual and intimate partner violence. Their journalistic writing focuses on sex, sexuality, gender and politics.*

Transphobia – and attacks on trans lives – has become one of the most important human rights issues of our time. In the UK and America, what was once the fringe opinion of radicals of various ilks (a topic we'll explore briefly in this piece) has become a mainstream political talking point. In the UK, it is a bi-partisan tactic, levied by both the Conservatives and Labour. The Conservatives use transphobia as a cheap tactic to retain votes after 12 years of rule has eroded every public service in the UK down to its bones, causing the greatest dip in general quality of life since the 1950s (Partington, 2022). Meanwhile, Labour use transphobia as an attempt to win favour and build back the credibility it lost with middle-class liberals during the Corbyn era. In America, it is less of a bi-partisan issue but despite (and possibly, because of) power passing back into the hands of the Democrats in the 2021 election, Republican and far-right representatives have had huge success in rolling back trans rights and protections at state levels – most notably in Florida where there are sweeping restrictions on gender-affirming care, drag, teachers using correct pronouns for students, and bathroom usage.

In this chapter, we'll explore some of the origins of the TERF (trans-exclusionary radical feminist) ideology and how its emphasis on gender essentialism necessitates biphobia. We'll then move on to how the TERF movement has morphed into the "Gender Critical" movement, shedding much of its remnants of radicalism or feminism to align itself with the far right in order to attack not only the rights of trans people in the UK, but all queer people and women. While we'll touch on the biphobia of the Gender Critical movement – as this is a much under-discussed area – this second exploration will focus on how the bi community can unite against the threat of fascism.

* * *

Long before we were all stuck in our houses because of Covid-19, Britain was gripped by an entirely different outbreak.

Swathes of seemingly progressive women and feminists fell victim to a nasty bout of transphobia that swept through the press and population like wildfire. The spark – this time round – was changes proposed to the Gender Recognition Act, which would make it ever so slightly easier for trans people to be legally recognized as their gender, and which were brought forward in 2017. Opponents to this change claimed to have "legitimate concerns" over how it would affect women's rights and spaces. In actuality, many were using a technique popular among certain corners of the alt-right, notably Groypers, known as "Just asking questions" (sometimes memeified as "JAQing off") to undermine the legitimacy of a proposition or move the framing of the debate without providing any real counter-arguments. "By co-opting the language of women's rights and allying this with the tropes of 'legitimate concerns' and 'common sense', often with oblique references to 'science' or 'reality', trans-exclusionary feminism invokes reason and reasonability," writes Thurlow (2022).

For TERFs, the questions being asked were not about the ins and outs of how the state would recognize and legitimize gender identities (and in doing so create policy through which they were either protected or exploited), neither were they asking what right the state has to legitimize how a person identifies in the first place. Instead, the questions they asked sought to undermine the validity, dignity and even humanity of trans people by framing them as inherently dangerous. As Edie Miller writes for the Outline:

> Before long, though, [their transphobia...] developed an obsession: that trans women aren't actually women, and instead violent men intent on gaining access to women's bathrooms, prisons, and domestic violence shelters to harm them, and the idea that gender self-identification is ripe for abuse by cis men who claim to be trans. (Miller, 2018)

This wave of mainstream transphobia buoyed some very unexpected candidates to the top of the "radical feminist" ranks, with straight male comedians and anti-LGBT+ Catholics being touted as some of the key voices of those "defending lesbians" and "speaking up for women". As the movement progressed, connections between feminists and groups fundamentally opposed to bodily autonomy solidified, which we'll explore in the latter half of this chapter.

While trans people are the main and most vulnerable target of transphobic rhetoric in the UK, those who espouse it also take aim at anyone who threatens their binarist worldview, including bisexual women. Julie Bindel, a Political Lesbian, regularly dismisses bi women as "boring straight women using lesbianism to seem interesting" (2019), accuses bi women of treating their lesbian partners as fashion accessories, "For a straight woman, having a girlfriend on the side is almost like having the latest Prada handbag" (2012), and calls them "blue-fringed fake queers". Graham Lineham, who is heterosexual, has previously accused non-monosexual queer people of "land-grabbing gay liberation" (Shearing, 2018), and Sarah Ditum, a straight woman, voiced on Twitter (now known as X) that she finds the word bisexual "aggravating" because it "lumps men and women in together in a way that [she finds] pretty meaningless and v [sic] erasing of women" (Shearing, 2020).

So why would a group of people who claim to be fighting so hard to defend women, especially queer women, be so biphobic? Ditum's comment is actually the most illuminating answer. Bisexuality is a threat to TERF politics for three key reasons: it undermines the importance of gender differences, it undermines the idea that any woman would choose a man-free life if she could, and finally, it makes it much harder to construct a desexualized universalized essence of womanhood.

TERF ideology is, in part, the descendant of the same type of cultural feminism that grew out of the feminist sex wars of the 1970s. "The feminist sex wars" were debates about the role of sexuality in feminist politics. It was during this time that some Lesbian Feminists (it should be noted here that Lesbian Feminism is a specific branch of feminist theory and does not just refer to lesbians who are feminists) politicized lesbianism by framing it as an inherently feminist choice to live a man-free life. This move was in part a reaction to the lesbiphobia (and more general queerphobia) of cultural second-wave feminism, which saw lesbians and queer women as damaging to the cause of feminism; many cultural feminists at the time were keen to distance themselves from the stereotype that they were "man-hating lesbians", and were willing to throw queer women under the bus to do so. In response to this, Lesbian Feminists positioned lesbianism as the only way to be a real feminist, free from the brain-washing of the patriarchy. To do so, they suggested lesbianism is a choice any woman could and should make, thus Political Lesbianism and lesbian separatism was born. This is a very brief and slightly reductive overview of the emergence of political lesbianism, which has been the occupying topic of many in-depth and insightful explorations. It should also be noted that TERF ideology is influenced by the White Feminism and twee femonationalism that has been so prevalent within British feminism.

Political Lesbianism as a movement de-emphasized – to the point of erasing – sexual/romantic attraction to women as a core tenet, instead emphasizing decentring men as sexual or romantic partners. Paula Rust writes in the book *Bisexuality and the Challenge to Lesbian Politics*:

> Given the political lesbian's proximity to essential womanhood, her desexualization was a comfort to cultural feminists for two reasons. First, it purified her of embarrassing sexual habits that would tarnish her womanly image [...] because sexuality

itself was vulgar and unwomanly. Second, it universalized her. By definition, woman essence must exist in every woman. [...] Because of her political nature, her sexual purity, and her universality, the political lesbian became cultural feminism's prototypical woman. (1995, p.229)

Bisexuals do not fit into the TERF worldview because we are much harder to desexualize and universalize than Political Lesbians. Our existence makes it much more difficult to argue that the differences between sexes and genders are important and wide enough to make desire for both (because TERFs also refuse to acknowledge the existence of non-binary people) incompatible, and our decision to continue to identify as bi even when we could only date women undermines the argument that any woman would live free of men if only she were able to. As Rust writes in the same text:

[Bisexuality] challenges the feminist valuation of women in the same way that lesbians themselves challenge the male supremacist valuation of men. [The bisexual woman] belies the lesbian feminist argument that in a sexist society lesbian relations are inherently superior to heterosexual relations because she has had the opportunity to experience both and she does not agree. (1995, p.276)

It's important to note that in this quote, "lesbian" refers to a woman who prioritizes relationships with women over relationships with men, rather than a woman who is attracted to women.

Mostly, TERF biphobia is no different from run-of-the-mill monosexism. Because bisexuality destabilizes the category of "men" and "women" and "gay" and "straight", making it harder to argue that those categories need their own separate spaces, TERF ideology tries to erase and demonize us. Kenji Yoshino, in "The epistemic contract of bisexual Erasure", writes:

> [D]oes bisexuality, which stereotypically does not pass desire through the lens of sex, threaten human identity? [...] it can be noted that bisexuality, like intersexuality, suggests that the question 'Is it a boy or a girl?' is the wrong question to be asking. And if this is the question that determines our humanity, it should come as no surprise that the capacity of bisexuals to undermine the sex category is deeply threatening to individuals of all categories. (2000, p.413)

This is another area where biphobia and transphobia overlap; both are – in some ways – rooted in fear of ambiguity, fluidity, and transcending of categorization. The existence of trans people shows that the categories of man and woman are not as binary or distinct as cishet society would have us believe. You can move from one to the other. You can be neither or both. You can be something else entirely. Bisexuality plays a similar role with sexuality. Both, too, bring queerness closer to home and undermine the idea that showing attraction to the "other gender/sex" is not enough to disprove any accusations of queerness. A partnership that may look heterosexual from the outside may be made up of people who are bi and/or trans. Not only do we blur the lines of gay and straight, man and women, our existence obfuscates the line distinction between "queer" and "not". This argument is the basis of Yoshino's (2000) epistemic contract. To further this, Garelick and colleagues (2017) argue that groups predisposed to religious fundamentalism and authoritarianism (and TERFs and Gender Critical are an authoritarian movement) may be more likely to be biphobic and transphobic:

It can be argued that those with a higher need for structure may be particularly discomfited by individuals who are bisexual and who are transgender, compared to individuals who are gay/lesbian, because of the mistaken belief that bisexuality and transgenderism inevitably involve fluidity of sexual and/or gender identity and, thus, a destabilization of the social structures of sexuality and gender. (Garelick et al., 2017, p.176)

Later in the study, they go on to say that in further investigations, they would expect to see "those who explicitly endorse binary views of gender and sexuality to show the highest levels of biphobia and transphobia, but not homophobia" (p.185).

Further, it is not just heterosexual society that has felt threatened by these challenges to gender and sexual binaries. As bi and trans activist and author Julia Serano (2012) points out, "Historically, transgender and bisexual activists often saw themselves on the same side of challenging exclusion within greater gay and lesbian communities and organizations." In an essay proceeding that one, Serano (2010) reminds us that bi and trans people have historically faced exclusion from gay and lesbian spaces for similar reasons:

While the reasons for bisexual and transgender exclusion from lesbian and gay communities during the '70s and '80s may be somewhat different, the rhetoric used to cast us away was eerily similar: We, in one way or another, were supposedly "buying into" and "reinforcing" heteronormativity.

Bi people are a threat to TERF politics because we do not fit into their worldview that sex is the most important defining characteristic of identity and, because of this, a woman's identity is inherently different (and purer) than a man's. We also undermine their argument that all women both need and want the option to be completely free from maleness (as defined by sex and not gender) if possible.

As the tide of mainstream transphobia in the UK has risen, it has begun to break its banks and spill out into more generalized anti-queer rhetoric. Examples include the uncritical platforming of people like Caroline Farrow, an anti-LGBTQ+ Catholic activist, and the movement's links to America's Christian Right. In recent years, this movement mutated from an arguably fringe rupture within feminist politics to an overarching "culture war", which sought to roll back the rights and civil liberties of trans people in the UK. This change is best represented by the movement's rebranding from self-referring as TERFs, to "Gender Critical". Thurlow (2022) argues that the adoption of this name "represented the beginnings of a pivot by trans-exclusionary feminists towards language which obscures their trans-exclusionary focus". For some, it also represents a move away from the radical feminist roots of the movement towards a more nakedly conservative campaign, one which makes alignment with Evangelicals and Catholic lobbyists – as well as far-right groups like Turning Point UK, Patriotic Alternative and The Proud Boys – more viable. More recently, Gender Critical activists such as Posie Parker (Kellie-Jay Keen-Minshull) have expressed their support for far-right groups who attend anti-Drag Queen Story Hours protests or Let Women Speak events (Ore, 2023).

The Gender Critical movement is also more openly anti-LGBTQIA+ than its predecessor. Many in the movement virulently oppose Drag Queen Story Hours – an initiative in which drag performers read children's books in public libraries and venues – claiming that these will "indoctrinate children", or, worse, calling drag performers "groomers". This rhetoric mirrors that of Section 28, which all but banned any positive discussions or representation of queer identities in public life for 15 years. In the lead-up to the passing of Section 28 in 1988 by Tory prime minister Margaret Thatcher, queer men in particular were demonized in the media as being a danger to children, and queer sexuality was conflated with paedophilia. The HIV epidemic also played a key role, as cis heterosexual society feared this new disease and the possibility that someone could become sick simply from being in proximity to queer people.

Another clear-cut comparison is the demonization of children's books which depict queerness. In 1983, Susanne Bösche published *Jenny Lives with Eric and Martin*, a picture book about a young girl who lives with her dad and his boyfriend. "No one could foresee the negative impact that this story would have on 1980's England. In 1986, not long before the introduction of Section 28, a newspaper reported that a copy of the book was on display in the library of a London primary school," writes LGBT Lawyers (2021). Today, groups are organizing not only against Drag Queen Story Hours, but around the banning of books about queerness aimed at children.

The movement has also become more dedicated to gender essentialism. However, this does not stem *from* its radical feminist roots, but rather *away* from them. Not only do Gender Criticals reject wholesale the notion that it is possible to change sex (as the name suggests, they reject the idea of gender as something separate to sex), they have become increasingly fervent in policing traditional gender roles in regard to dress – notably through their policing of the gender expressions of anyone trying to use a public toilet. Thus, not only does the Gender Critical movement threaten bisexuals through attacks on LGBTQIA+ rights and lives, any movement built around gender essentialism is inherently exclusionary of bisexuality, which by its nature eludes and transverses the concept of inherent, distinct gender binarism.

As has been explored in other texts (although not as much as it could have been), the overlap between transphobia and biphobia – particularly their shared roots in challenging the gender binary – is not just theoretical. There is significant overlap between bi and trans communities. First, there is a large overlap in the demographics themselves: one-third (32 per cent) of respondents to the 2015 US Transgender Survey (James *et al.*, 2016) identified as bisexual or pansexual, compared to 16 per cent who identified as lesbian or gay and 15 per cent as heterosexual. Second, our material realities also overlap significantly, which Jacob Engelberg (2022) explores in his article "There is no sexual liberation without bisexuals", writing:

> Contemporary trans politics focuses on issues like healthcare, homelessness, workplace discrimination and sexual violence – material inequities that affect our social groups in an overlapping fashion. The fact that, according to the most recent government figures from 2017, the majority of trans people in the UK identify as bi- or pansexual (45.7%) should reinforce those connections.

Indeed, several studies have shown that bisexuals face higher rates of sexual violence and poverty, have worse health outcomes, and are less likely to be in gainful employment than straight or gay people. A further example comes again from the 2015 US Transgender Survey, which found that "[b]isexual and pansexual transgender respondents were more likely to live in poverty than were both gay and lesbian and heterosexual transgender people" (Movement Advancement Project, 2017, p.2). Engelberg (2022) goes on to argue that "It's here that bisexual politics has a natural alliance with trans politics, as it did during the 1990s."

The goal of this exploration of the biphobia innate in the TERF and Gender Critical movements – as well as the overlap of trans and biphobia – is not to try to claim that biphobia is the reason why we – as bisexuals – should mobilize against it, but rather to provide an ideological framework on which to build a way to oppose it. For example, much has been written about how both movements harm lesbians in their weaponization of lesbian identities to justify their transphobia and transmisogyny. Many examples could be given here, from their arguments that "trans activism erases lesbians" to groups such as The Lesbian Project (co-founded by Julie Bindel and Kathleen Stock) and Get The L Out (the group that gatecrashed Pride in London in 2018 in protest of trans inclusion). In response, the lesbian community has mobilized to oppose these arguments, notably via groups such as The Dyke Project (launched in 2023 to counter The Lesbian Project), LWithTheT, and other grassroots community groups. In order to do this, lesbian communities sought to understand the TERF and Gender Critical ideological beliefs around lesbianism and undermine these with vocal and organized support of trans people on the basis of their lesbianism, rather than in spite of it.

Let's get more granular to explore how the bi community might do this. In April 2023, the Equality and Human Rights Commission (EHRC) provided advice to the "Minister for Women and Equalities on the definition of the protected characteristic of 'sex' in the Equality Act 2010 (Equality and Human Rights Commission, 2023)". In this letter, the organization argued that "if 'sex' is defined as biological sex for the purposes of [Equalities Act 2010], this would bring greater legal clarity in eight areas", one of which was "Freedom of association for lesbians and gay men". In this paragraph, the EHRC appeared to create an argument that people are "legally" lesbians/gay men on the basis of their biological sex. Bisexuals are excluded from this argument that "sex" must be defined as biological in order to protect sexual minorities, as bisexuality transverses the idea of sexuality and gender being binary. The EHRC argues (falsely) that allowing trans women to be recognized as women would be a threat to female-exclusive lesbian spaces, but it does not conceive of any such gender-segregated bisexual spaces or the existence of any bisexual spaces at all. Later, the EHRC (2023) argues that "One instance where this is likely to make a difference is data on gay, lesbian and bisexual people. The removal of sex as a category risks erasing lesbians and gay men as meaningful categories for analysis." Despite being acknowledged in the previous sentence, bisexuals are – somewhat ironically – erased in the latter arguing for so-called protections of sexual minorities as a "meaningful category". This, I think, is very illuminating; does the EHRC not consider bisexuality to be a meaningful category? It appears not.

In instances like this, the bisexual movement could – indeed must – be exploiting the biphobia of the Gender Critical movement in order to advocate for and protect our trans siblings. We can do this by loudly and consistently leveraging our support for trans people on the basis of our bisexuality, and by continuing to challenge the monosexism that underpins the movement's worldview. This can be done a number of ways, including (but certainly not limited to) pushing back against the nominal use of bisexuality by groups such as the LGB Alliance; organizing bi blocs at trans rights protests; writing to MPs and parliamentary lobbying groups to point out how proposed changes such as those outlined above would harm bi people; contributing to pro-trans rights campaigns in way that is publically and visibility bisexual; and pushing back against respectability politics and transphobia within the bi community, making it impossible for us as a movement and community to be a tool for transphobic gain.

Prior to the pandemic, there was an organized and mobilized response to the rising threat of transphobia in the UK from the bisexual community. Groups such as London Bi Pandas, Biscuit, the Bi Survivors Network, and BWithTheT (the latter two of which I organized) were organizing demos, bi blocs in trans rights protests and marches, creating resources, and aligning with trans, lesbian, feminist, and anti-facist groups to hold counter-demos wherever TERFs spoke or met.

But the bi movement has been slow to bounce back after two years of lockdown. Little attention has been paid to this by the queer press or academia, but I would argue that the economic impact on a demographic who are more likely to have been living in poverty previously – and whose movement receives the least amount of funding of any of the LGBT demographics from LGBT funders – has left us struggling to procure the resources with which to organize. As well as this, studies from America (Griffis, 2022) suggest that bi and trans people are more likely to be suffering from long Covid (another example of our material overlap). While grassroots actions are our most effective tool, the bi community needs more support from queer organizations such as Stonewall, in order to more effectively mobilize.

In 2019, only a few months before the pandemic struck, I organized a demo via BWithTheT and alongside LWithTheT and London Bi Pandas in protest of the LGB Alliance's formation. In an article written at the time for Dazed (Abraham, 2019), I am quoted as saying that we were creating counter-messaging because "it's the right thing to do". Despite undoubtedly being infuriating for the journalist who was trying to interview me between setting up banners and organizing speakers, I stand by this reasoning. We must continue to fight for trans rights not because of the biphobia, lesbiphobia, homophobia and every other prejudice inherent in the TERF and Gender Critical movements (of which there are many), but because trans rights are human rights, and defending the rights of vulnerable minorities is the right thing to do. Trans people are entitled to humanity, dignity, safety, shelter, joy and healthcare because we are all entitled to those things.

But the biphobia of the TERF and Gender Critical movements is also one of our strongest tools for how we can continue to undermine them as a community. We make up the largest demographic of the queer community and our existence undermines several key tenets of Gender Critical arguments. We must be resolute in challenging their ideal version of womanhood as desexualized and purified of male essence. We must support other groups threatened by TERF and Gender Critical rhetoric and advocate for bodily autonomy. We must push back against bio-essentialism and celebrate the diversity of womanhood, of our genitals, our desires and our choices.

References

Abraham, A. (2019). "Activists are protesting a group that wants to drop the T from LGBT." Dazed. www.dazeddigital.com/life-culture/article/46586/1/how-people-are-defying-a-new-transphobic-hate-group.

Bindel, J. (2012). "Where's the politics in sex?" HuffPost, 12 June 2012. www.huffpost.com/entry/where-is-the-politics-in_b_1589435.

Bindel, J. (2019). "Why are boringly straight women claiming to be lesbians?" *The Spectator*, 5 June 2019. www.spectator.co.uk/article/why-are-boringly-straight-women-claiming-to-be-lesbians.

Bösche, S. (1983). *Jenny Lives with Eric and Martin*. London: Gay Men's Press.

Engelberg, J. (2022). "There is no sexual liberation without bisexuals." Novara Media, 14 February 2022. novaramedia.com/2022/02/14/there-is-no-sexual-liberation-without-bisexuals.

Equality and Human Rights Commission. (2023). Clarifying the definition of "sex" in the Equality Act. 4 April 2023. https://www.equalityhumanrights.com/media-centre/news/clarifying-definition-sex-equality-act.

Garelick, A.S., Filip-Crawford, G., Varley, A.H., Nagoshi, C.T., Nagoshi, J.L. & Evans, R. (2017). Beyond the binary: Exploring the role of ambiguity in biphobia and transphobia. *Journal of Bisexuality*, 17(2), 172–189.

Griffis, M. (2022). "Long COVID Is More Common in Bisexual and Trans People. The Reasons Why Are Complicated." Them, 27 July 2022. www.them.us/story/long-covid-trans-and-bisexual-people-healthcare-disparities.

James, S.E., Herman, J.L., Rankin, S., Keisling, M., Mottet, L. & Anafi, M. (2016). *The Report of the 2015 US Transgender Survey*. Washington, DC: National Center for Transgender Equality.

LGBT Lawyers. (2021). "Section 28: History, Response and Impact." lgbtlawyers.co.uk/2021/02/08/section-28.

Miller, E. (2018). "Why is British media so transphobic?" The Outline, 5 November 2018. https://theoutline.com/post/6536/british-feminists-media-transphobic?zd=1&zi=ynrzjjam.

Movement Advancement Project. (2017). *A Closer Look: Bisexual Transgender People*. www.lgbtmap.org/file/A%20Closer%20Look%20Bisexual%20Transgender.pdf.

Ore, Adeshola. "Victoria to Ban Nazi Salute after "Disgusting" Scenes at Anti-Trans Protest." *The Guardian*, 19 Mar. 2023, www.theguardian.com/australia-news/2023/mar/20/victoria-to-ban-nazi-salute-after-anti-trans-protest-melbourne-australia. Accessed 24 Mar. 2024.

Partington, R. (2022). "UK households face biggest fall in living standards since 1950s, say experts." *The Guardian*, 26 February 2022. www.theguardian.com/business/2022/feb/26/uk-households-face-biggest-fall-in-living-standards-since-1950s-say-experts.

Rust, P.C. (1995). *Bisexuality and the Challenge to Lesbian Politics: Sex, Loyalty, and Revolution*. New York, NY: New York University Press.

Serano, J. (2010). "Bisexuality does not reinforce the gender binary." Bi Radical. bidyke.tumblr.com/post/15612928872/julia-serano-bisexuality-does-not-reinforce-the.

Serano. J. (2012). "Bisexuality and binaries revisited." Whipping Girl, 19 November 2012. juliaserano.blogspot.com/2012/11/bisexuality-and-binaries-revisited.html.

Shearing, L. (2018). "No, bi people are not 'appropriating gay culture'." Medium, 14 August 2018. https://medium.com/@lois.shearing/no-bi-people-are-not-appropriating-gay-culture-6102d6638f45.

Shearing, L. (2020). "Why bisexuality is a threat to TERF politics." Medium, 2 April 2020. https://medium.com/@lois.shearing/why-bisexuality-is-a-threat-to-terf-politics-5f2b40563e11.

Thurlow, C. (2022). From TERF to gender critical: A telling genealogy? *Sexualities*. https://doi.org/10.1177/13634607221107827.

Yoshino, K. (2000). The epistemic contract of bisexual erasure. *Stanford Law Review*, 52(2), 353.

Further reading

Harrison, J. (2013). "Wonky Wednesday: Trans people & sexual orientation." National LGBTQ Task Force, 5 June 2013. www.thetaskforce.org/wonky-wednesday-trans-people-sexual-orientation.

Michaelson, J. (2016). "Radical feminists and Conservative Christians team up against transgender people." Daily Beast, 4 September 2016. www.thedailybeast.com/radical-feminists-and-conservative-christians-team-up-against-transgender-people.

Parsons, V. (2000). "Anti-gay, anti-trans activist Caroline Farrow thinks NHS rainbow lanyards are a 'hostile political symbol'." Pink News, 6 March 2020. www.thepinknews.com/2020/03/06/caroline-farrow-nhs-rainbow-lanyards-badges-misogynistic-pride-lgbt-twitter.

Stonewall. (2017). "What does the UK Government announcement on the Gender Recognition Act mean?" Stonewall, 13 October 2017. https://web.archive.org/web/20230604133037/www.stonewall.org.uk/what-does-uk-government-announcement-gender-recognition-act-mean.

CHAPTER 9

What If We Weren't Born That Way?

Heron Greenesmith

This piece was originally published in Extramagazine.com.

Heron Greenesmith (they/them) is a policy attorney from Massachusetts, USA. Currently monitoring the anti-LGBTQ right wing for Political Research Associates, Heron is also adjunct faculty at Boston University School of Law, and the co-founder of BiLaw and the Polyamory Legal Advocacy Coalition. Heron's piece about immutability and bisexuality first appeared in Teen Vogue *magazine and represents a lifetime of thinking about sexual orientation and the human experience. Heron is a polyamorous agender bisexual parent with two cats.*

In 1989, my best friend in second grade gave me a diamond necklace and asked me to marry him. (I don't think it was a real diamond – was it, Raymond?) My mother made me return it and decline his offer. In 1992, I unzipped my friend's jumpsuit as we were standing in line to go to lunch. I remember the feeling of the tab between my finger and thumb. She was horrified. I got sent to the office.

Two years later, I lay in my bed every night and whispered my crush's name, hoping he'd hear me across the kilometres of city street noise between us. And in 2002, in my college apartment above a pizza shop and full of strange feelings for my best girl friend, I wondered to myself: "Am I bisexual?"

I *am* bisexual. But was I bisexual in 1989? In 1992? In 1994? Was I born bisexual? Did I come out of the closet, or did my identity evolve?

Does it matter?

My identity and experience, after all, aren't uncommon. More than half of LGBTQ2S+ adults in America are bisexual, according to a recent Gallup survey (Jones, 2022). And increasing percentages of people, especially young ones, are finding words beyond "gay" and "straight" to define their sexuality, such as queer, pan, ace and so on (and, like me, they are similarly embracing non-binary gender identities, too).

In the summer of 2020, actor Niecy Nash married musician Jessica Betts. Nash's two previous marriages were to men and she had happily considered herself straight, until she fell in love with Betts. Yet Nash has refused to call this a "coming out". "I wasn't anywhere to come out of," she said. "I wasn't living a sexually repressed life when I was married to men. I just loved them when I loved them. And now, I love her," she said of Betts (Cuby, 2021).

These kinds of expressions of sexual fluidity and change might not align with the popular narratives of being born either gay or straight, or of coming out as queer after a miserable existence within the closet, but they are no less real. For many of us, the why of our sexuality just isn't as important as the how: how can we live as we are with autonomy, safety and joy?

To those on the anti-LGBTQ2S+ right, however, the *why* does matter. A lot. And that is a problem.

Back in 1938 (no, this part isn't about me and my crushes), US Supreme Court Justice Harlan Stone wrote a seemingly innocuous note in a case deciding whether the federal government could intervene in the regulation of the transport of milk products – a footnote that would change US law (Caplan, 2013).

Yes, wrote Justice Stone, the federal legislative body could absolutely regulate interstate commerce without worrying about infringing on companies' due process rights. But, he added, the court would look very closely at any laws that would have an impact on a "discrete and insular minority", rather than a corporation. In other words, legislation that infringed the civil rights of minority groups could be subjected to higher scrutiny by courts to ensure those rights were upheld.

With those four words, Justice Stone paved the way for both landmark legal victories in the US, such as Brown v. Board of Education (Legal Defense Fund, 2023), and landmark legislation, including the Civil Rights Act and the Americans with Disabilities Act. In the past 30 years, this higher level of legal scrutiny has been the basis for the federal litigation that has enshrined marriage equality and non-discrimination protections for LGBTQ2S+ people in the US.

But in the process, US jurisprudence incidentally established a legal mechanism for civil rights that relies on a key term: immutability – a quality or attribute that is fixed and cannot be altered. In order to qualify as a "discrete and insular minority", the court said in another case, a group must meet certain criteria, such as having faced historical discrimination based on a shared characteristic and not having access to traditional methods of political power. And, most significantly for my argument, the shared characteristic must be immutable (McBride, 2019).

And so, when gay, lesbian and, to some extent, bisexual people began to seek legal protection from discrimination on the basis of sexual orientation in the US and elsewhere in the 1980s and 1990s, they picked up the "born this way" baton to attempt to prove that sexual orientation is an immutable trait. If being gay couldn't be changed, the reasoning went, then gay people deserved protections and rights.

In 2010, for example, during a trial to overturn Proposition 8 (The Perry Case Transcripts), a 2008 ballot initiative that banned same-sex marriage in California, lawyer Ted Olson led plaintiff Sandy Stier through an explanation of her relationship history. Stier was partnered with a woman whom she hoped to marry, but previously had been married to a man.

In order to show that prohibiting marriage equality was discriminatory, Olson felt he had to establish that Stier would be harmed by being able to only marry people of a different gender. But how could that be true if she had already married a man? Why couldn't she just marry another man and be happy?

Let's look at how the line of questioning sets up a gay-straight binary, and posits Stier's marriage to a man as something inauthentic compared to her authentic feelings for her female partner:

Olson: Are you saying that you weren't in love with your husband?

Stier: I was not in love with my husband, no.

Olson: Did you think that you were at some point?

Stier: I had a hard time relating to the concept of being in love when I was married to my husband. And while I did love him when I married him, I honestly just couldn't relate when people said they were in love. I thought they were overstating their feelings and maybe making a really big deal out of something. It didn't really make sense to me. It seemed dramatic.

Olson: How convinced are you that you are gay? You've lived with a husband. You said you loved him. Some people might say, "Well, it's this and then it's that and it could be this again." Answer that.

Stier: Well, I'm convinced, because at 47 years old I have fallen in love one time and it's with Kris. And our love is – it's a blend of many things. It's physical attraction. It's romantic attraction. It's a strong commitment. It's intellectual bonding and emotional bonding. For me, it just isn't love. I really, quite frankly, don't know what that would be for adults. I don't know what else to say about it.

I'm not saying that Stier loved her husband more than she admitted, nor am I saying that she is bisexual. But I do know people who have deeply loved men and then went on to deeply love women (and vice versa), and those people should have the right to marry whomever they want, whatever their gender. Olson's line of questioning, however, places bisexuality and fluidity as enemies of the freedom to marry, as inconveniences that might threaten a careful legal strategy.

(It's worth noting alternative judicial thinking when it comes to the matter of immutability. In 1995, the Supreme Court of Canada ruled in the landmark Egan v. Canada, which established sexual orientation as a prohibited basis of discrimination under section 15 of the Canadian Charter of Rights and Freedoms. On the question of whether rights should only be extended on the basis of immutable characteristics, Canadian Supreme Court Justice Gérard La Forest wrote:

I have no difficulty accepting the appellants' contention that whether or not sexual orientation is based on biological or physiological factors, which may be a matter of some controversy, it is a deeply personal characteristic that is either unchangeable or changeable only at unacceptable personal costs.

In other words: the cause or source of one's identity is irrelevant in deciding whether rights should be extended.)

The result of hitching our rights to the idea that our identities are fixed is that the immutability of sexual orientation (and, likewise, gender identity) has now been solidly entrenched in the American legal and cultural milieux. National Coming Out Day celebrates a singular event, while ignoring the reality of prolonged and multiple experiences of coming out, of shifts back into closets of safety and of changes in sexual orientation and gender identity over time. It's still common to hear queer people speak of their sexuality as something they wouldn't have picked for themselves if they had had a choice – a fairly damning and depressing view of our vibrant communities. After all, what's wrong with choosing queerness?

As long as there have been expressions and experiences of desire outside the hetero norm, there have also been forces bent on eradicating them: from prayers and exorcism, shame and rejection, to institutionalization, imprisonment and violence. It's understandable, then, that for some gay rights advocates – especially those who feel that their own sexual orientation is innate – the best case to make for tolerance and acceptance is to argue that homosexuality is natural and inherent, not an aberration but a variation.

The problem is that many LGBTQ2S+ activists invested far too much in an argument that is both false and a dead end: queerness isn't immutable for all of us. Queerness can be beautifully fluid.

There's plenty of evidence to back this up. In her 2008 study on the fluidity of sexual orientation, American psychologist Lisa Diamond found that 67 per cent of sexual-minority women changed the label of their sexual orientation over a period of ten years (Diamond, 2008). And LGBTQ2S+ health researcher Sabra Katz-Wise (2012), in a similar study, found that 64 per cent of women and 52 per cent of men surveyed reported a change in their attraction to other people. "Sexuality is fluid", one queer woman in the study told Katz-Wise. "I just happen to go for particular genders at particular times, and I feel like that's pretty normal. Plus, of course I'll feel more gay if I'm dating a woman than if I'm dating a man, that's just how that works."

But can the law also be fluid in how it recognizes the reality of sexual orientation? Some legal scholars and judges have explored the flexibility of immutability, to coin a phrase. Does immutability insist on the *inability* to change, or, as a judge has phrased it, on "traits that are so central to a person's identity that it would be abhorrent for a government to penalize a person for refusing to change them, regardless of how easy that change might be physically" (Clarke, 2015)? In other words, is an immutable characteristic one that a person is unable to change, or one that it would be wrong to force someone to change?

Professor Diamond and law professor Clifford J. Rosky are at the forefront of a movement to transform how sexual orientation is understood in law. They wrote a paper in 2016 that laid bare the flaws of immutability: it's unscientific, it isn't relevant in protecting people from discrimination and it implies that some forms of attraction are less valid than others. To Diamond and Rosky, "now that the U.S. Constitution grants every individual the unfettered liberty to choose same-sex relationships, it simply does not matter why these choices are made and whether they were influenced by genes, hormones, society or chance" (2016, p.32).

It's worth noting here that many other commonly protected characteristics and identities are not immutable in the "unchangeable" sense of the word. For example, discrimination on the basis of religion is prohibited, including toward those who have converted to a religion. Disability status can change multiple times over a lifetime, and there exist protections for disabled people. And, finally, race, which is a protected characteristic, is itself a social construct that white supremacists have an investment in maintaining and expanding or contracting in order to keep the sanctity of whiteness.

Yet the supposed immutability of sexual orientation still rests at the heart of the legal strategy to expand the freedom to marry and guarantee protections from discrimination. Consider this quote from US Supreme Court Justice Anthony Kennedy's opinion in Obergefell v. Hodges, which brought marriage equality to the United States: The "immutable nature [of sexual orientation] dictates that same-sex marriage is their only real path to this profound commitment" (Wayback Machine, 2014, p.4).

And so we have two diverging roads: the reality of fluidity in sexual orientation (and gender identity), and the legal necessity of relying on the unscientific construct of immutability in order to further rights and protections for LGBTQ2S+ people.

Here is why we need to be wary: the anti-LGBTQ2S+ conservative movement is watching all of this very closely. In 2019, Peter Sprigg, of the fundamentalist Christian lobby group Family Research Council, wrote a paper titled "Evidence shows that sexual orientation can change: Debunking the myth of 'immutability'". In this article, he facetiously endorses the call by pro-LGB scholars Lisa Diamond and Clifford Rosky to "abandon the immutability argument once and for all". Sprigg doesn't support Diamond and Rosky's position in any way other than to agree that "immutable" is an improper descriptor for sexual orientation. But Sprigg has nefarious ends – including denying LGBTQ2S+ people civil rights and advocating for conversion therapy. According to him, the fluidity of sexual orientation means that it should not be a basis for protection under law, and conversion therapy should be widely practised. His reasoning is that if sexual orientation *can* change over time, people should be able to work with a therapist to facilitate that change.

But all the therapists that the Family Research Council supports believe that everyone should only change one way: towards being straight. And to get their clients there, these therapists use "non-affirming" techniques, including, in some cases, literal torture (Sprigg, 2019; Office of the High Commissioner for Human Rights, 2020).

Rhetoric like Sprigg's is finding sympathetic ears, particularly from those who are transphobic and opposed to transgender rights and gender critical parents of trans children, who wish to suppress their children's identity through non-affirming therapies.

Another Christian right-wing activist, Glenn Stanton of Focus on the Family, has used the results of the recent Gallup survey on LGBTQ demographics to make a similar case against queer and trans rights. Writing in *The Federalist*, a mainstay Christian-right publication, he says, "The new data tell us people are simply becoming more elastic in how they view their sexuality and gender. And if sexuality is elastic, that has huge implications."

What are these huge implications? That's an excellent question that Stanton doesn't answer, aside from warning ominously that it is "becoming increasingly fashionable to be seen as sexually experimental today, evidenced in the fact that 55 percent of those who told Gallup they were 'LGBT' said they were bisexual".

And this is exactly why the "born that way" case for rights

is a dangerous one – because it leaves people with fluid identities vulnerable to discrimination, exclusion and harm. As long as the primary legal and moral argument for queer and trans rights is based on immutable and either/or characteristics, it will exclude those who are fluid, bisexual and non-binary. As long as the foundation of trans and queer rights is the belief that everyone's sexual orientation and gender identity are inherent and fixed, there will be gatekeepers of our identities.

Some of that gatekeeping will be judgement and derision within our own communities. And some of it will come from courts, educational institutions, governments, religious organizations and hate groups. If LGBTQ2S+ rights are *only* recognized on the basis of immutable characteristics, then Christian conservative groups and other anti-queer and anti-trans forces will continue to make headway by arguing that if people can change they should. Those of us who are able to prove we were, indeed, "born that way" might be okay, but those of us who can't – or won't – will be in danger of being forced into conversion therapy, denied affirming healthcare or refused civil rights protections.

In the face of the current anti-trans and anti-queer onslaught in the US and across the globe, it might be tempting to lean into the immutable characteristic argument to demand our right to be free from discrimination, but we must resist. Instead, the solution is to assert, as Diamond and Rosky (2016) do, that it simply does not matter whether our orientation or gender identity is influenced by genes, hormones, society, chance – or even God. We should fight for all people to be housed, clothed, fed, loved and kept healthy and well, regardless of who they are and how and why they got that way.

This is the foundation of justice: not "Tell the court why you shouldn't be kicked out of your house," but "We, as a society, believe that everyone should have a house." After all, why should we have to prove our legitimacy to the state in order to obtain basic human rights, such as freedom, equality, safety and dignity?

And yet, the state continues to control its citizens in ways that prevent us from surviving or thriving. As Andy Izenson, the legal director of the New York-based Chosen Family Law Center, told me, "The state seeks to control the bodies of its constituents: whether they are caged or free, where they may go, what they are, how they are used, what they are understood to be for."

Izenson points to examples such as punitive incarceration; non-consensual surgeries on intersex infants; restrictions on reproductive healthcare; the rigidity of a particular gender narrative required to access insurance coverage for affirming medical care; interpersonal violence against visibly gender-non-conforming individuals; and the capitalist devaluation of care, sex and domestic work.

"Embodying fluidity," Izenson continued, "is one tactic in resisting control." What better way to re-establish autonomy and agency than to reject imposed and rigid definitions of identity? What better path to freedom than to embrace expansiveness and possibility of change and choice? And what better way for a democracy to protect its residents than to denounce binaries in favour of justice?

As new generations lead the way towards embracing identities that are more fluid and less fixed, legal systems must follow suit or risk entrenching discrimination against LGBTQ2S+ people. A broad and nuanced understanding of sexual orientation and gender identity would defang support for conversion therapy and against non-discrimination protections.

A fluidity-inclusive ban on conversion therapy, for example, would acknowledge that many people experience shifts in their gender identity or sexual orientation over time, and that any effort to suppress that fluidity or direct someone towards a cisgender, heterosexual identity are unethical. A fluidity-inclusive non-discrimination law would assert that everyone has a gender identity and a sexual orientation, and that we all have a right to be free from discrimination based on those characteristics, regardless of how we might identify at any time.

Immutability is a trap with immeasurable power; it's a trap with the tantalizing allure of a life without discrimination, but it is a false promise. As long as some of us are seen as inauthentic or illegitimate, we are all at risk of being denied our rights and our humanity. We are not a monolith; not of race, religion, family creation, ability, class, sexuality or gender. Our strength is in our diversity and our way forward is to insist on equity, not deservingness.

References

Caplan, L. (2013). "Ruth Bader Ginsburg and Footnote Four." The New Yorker, 13 September 2013. www.newyorker.com/news/news-desk/ruth-bader-ginsburg-and-footnote-four.

Clarke, J.A. (2015). Against immutability. *Yale Law Journal*, 125(1), 2.

Cuby, M. (2021). "Niecy Nash doesn't feel the need to label her sexuality." Them, 11 March. 2021. www.them.us/story/niecy-nash-sexuality-labels-ellen-degeneres.

Diamond, L.M. (2008). Female bisexuality from adolescence to adulthood: Results from a 10-year longitudinal study. *Developmental Psychology*, 44(1), 5–14.

Diamond, L.M. & Rosky, C.R. (2016). Scrutinizing immutability: Research on sexual orientation and U.S. legal advocacy for sexual minorities. *Journal of Sex Research*, 53(4–5), 363–391.

Egan v. Canada [1995] Supreme Court of Canada. https://scc-csc.lexum.com/scc-csc/scc-csc/en/item/1265/index.do.

Jones, J. (2021). "LGBT identification rises to 5.6% in latest U.S. estimate." Gallup, 24 February 2021. https://news.gallup.com/poll/329708/lgbt-identification-rises-latest-estimate.aspx.

Katz-Wise, S. (2012). *Beyond Labels: Sexual Fluidity and Sexual Identity Development in Sexual Minority Young Adults.* PhD thesis, University of Wisconsin.

Legal Defense Fund. (2023). "Case: Brown v. Board of Education." Legal Defense and Educational Fund, 22 January 2019. www.naacpldf.org/case-issue/landmark-brown-v-board-education.

McBride, A. (2019). "The Supreme Court. Expanding Civil Rights. Landmark Cases. Frontiero v. Richardson (1973)." Thirteen PBS." www.thirteen.org/wnet/supremecourt/rights/landmark_frontiero.html.

Office of the High Commissioner for Human Rights (2020). "Conversion therapy" can amount to torture and should be banned says UN expert. 13 July 2020. www.ohchr.org/en/stories/2020/07/conversion-therapy-can-amount-torture-and-should-be-banned-says-un-expert.

The Perry Case Transcripts. American Foundation for Equal Rights. Afer.org, afer.org/our-work/hearing-transcripts.

Sprigg, P. (2019). *Evidence shows sexual orientation can change: Debunking the myth of "Immutability."* Washington, DC: Family Research Council.

Stanton, G.T. (2021). "Huge increase in LGBT identification casts doubt on 'born this way'." web.archive.org/web/20210302133559/thefederalist.com/2021/03/02/huge-increase-in-lgbt-identification-casts-doubt-on-born-this-way-claim.

"Wayback Machine." (2014) Obergefell et al. v. Hodges. Supreme Court of the United States. web.archive.org/web/20210211020838/www.supremecourt.gov/opinions/14pdf/14-556_3204.pdf.

Further reading

Baird, R. (2021). "The invention of whiteness: The long history of a dangerous idea." *The Guardian*, 20 April 2021. www.theguardian.com/news/2021/apr/20/the-invention-of-whiteness-long-history-dangerous-idea.

"California Proposition 8, Same-Sex Marriage Ban Initiative (2008)." (2008). BallotPedia, https://ballotpedia.org/California_Proposition_8,_Same-Sex_Marriage_Ban_Initiative_(2008).

Drmay, S. (2021). "What Demi Lovato's non-binary revelation means for the LGBTQ community." CBC, 21 May 2021. www.cbc.ca/news/entertainment/demi-lovato-non-binary-1.6036162.

Greenesmith, H. (2020). "Gender Critical Support Board Promotes Therapists Who Reject Transgender Identities." Teen Vogue, 17 June 2020. www.teenvogue.com/story/gender-critical-support-board-trans-youth.

Lhooq, M. (2016). "Meet the 72-year-old preacher behind one of the greatest gay club anthems of all time." Vice, 11 October 2016. www.vice.com/en/article/qkaw5p/carl-bean-born-this-way-lady-gaga-gay-club-anthem-national-coming-out-day.

CHAPTER 10

Where Fatness and Bisexuality Meet

Discipline and Anglo-American Capitalism

Maz Hedgehog

Maz Hedgehog (they/them) is a writer and performer generally working somewhere between poetry and theatre. Co-founder of theatre company Ink and Curtain, their work is lyrical and imaginative, frequently Inspired by folklore and mythology. Their latest book, The Body in its Seasons, *was published by Burning Eye Books in April 2022. Find them across the socials @MazHedgehog.*

One of the core myths of Anglo-American capitalism is the Protestant Work Ethic. The belief that Britain and America earned the wealth hoarded by their ruling classes through hard work, delayed gratification and careful discipline is a powerful one. It was born of post-Reformation patriarchy and white supremacy, providing intellectual justification for the colonial and industrial wealth acquisition of the 18th and 19th centuries. However, this mentality extended far beyond the fence around a plantation or the factory owner's front door, seeping into every aspect of the Anglo-American psyche.

The "Work Ethic" and its presumed moral superiority taught

these countries and these cultures that discipline could be projected onto everything. Just as settlers and imperialists brought other nations and the land they occupied under their control, they believed – and continue to believe – that people's bodies and desires could be similarly tamed. Anglo-American capitalism presumes that everything can be made predictable, coherent and reliable. Like an industrial loom or set of train tracks, capitalism believes that human beings, with their endless variation of bodies and desires and needs, can be turned into an asset, providing endless growth and limitless profits.

This, of course, is a fiction, and one which requires the subjugation of a wide range of states of being, including, but not limited to fatness, queer genders and sexualities, disability, old age and even death itself. This chapter will focus on fatness and bisexuality but the others cannot be ignored and any rounded view of anti-capitalism must take these into account.

Our societal preoccupation with becoming and remaining thin has precious little to do with taking care of people's wellbeing. Studies – such as one published in the *Annals of Internal Medicine* (Tsai & Thomas, 2005) – show that diet and weight loss plans almost never lead to long-term weight loss, with most regaining all the weight lost in a few years. This "weight cycling" does not produce positive health outcomes and has, in fact, been linked to higher mortality rates. Instead, the obsession with lifelong thinness is an obsession with the idea that our bodies can be made compliant. It says that by eating only the correct foods and moving in the proper ways, all bodies can be thin bodies. In the way of the Protestant Work Ethic and its associated asceticism – strict self-denial as a means of moral/ spiritual discipline – it turns taking pleasure in food into a sin and generates guilt and shame around eating "incorrectly". It says that fatness is a failure of self-control, the sign of a weak will. It produces diet culture, which says that by purchasing certain products (diet plans, superfoods, gym memberships, diet pills, weight loss surgery, etc.), "bad" fat bodies can be turned into "good" thin ones. It constructs thinness as the stable ideal against which fatness is defined as a temporary failing.

Similarly, heteronormativity teaches that desire can be controlled and contained. The dangerous pleasure of queerness, seen in its stereotyping as excessively hedonistic and hypersexual, is contrasted with the sedate responsibility of cisgender heterosexuality. Cis- and heteronormative communities are careful and vigilant in keeping queerness outside their boundaries. Intimacy is strictly policed, especially among men and people perceived as men, to ensure that no sign of queerness (and its associated potential for pleasure) is allowed to persist.

While most nice liberal spaces concede that homosexuality is a valid way of experiencing romantic love, it often does so with a narrative which reifies the boundaries between straight and not. "Born this way" rhetoric only really accepts queerness if it is entirely unavoidable and discrete from cisgender heterosexuality. It does little to push back against parenting mores which insist that children must be kept under strict control, or against social pressure for adults to adhere to set sexual scripts, lest they become or are read as gay.

Heteronormative life planning – get married/monogamously partnered, have children, work to provide for those children, and so on – is designed to create neat units of production. Contemporary nuclear families serve as easily identifiable categories to whom products can be sold, from whom profit is extracted and along which wealth passed on. Queer ways of creating kinship are less clear, less delineated and, therefore, less useful for capitalism. Heteronormativity, in part, enforces itself by insisting that there can be neat boundaries placed around desire, that sexuality is coherent and stable, that queerness can always be readily identified and marked out for punishment.

This need to systematize, to clearly separate out the "normal" from the "unnatural" and "disciplined" from the "immoral", does not stop at queerness. Bodies are similarly categorized and re-warded/punished. However, fatness shows that bodies cannot be tamed. The existence of fatness shows that bodies are des-tined to differentiate, to change size and shape as we grow and age. Fatness is therefore a sign that body size is not controllable. Whereas bisexuality, pansexuality and other multi-gender at-tractions show that desire cannot be tamed, that experiencing (apparently) heterosexual attraction does not preclude queer-ness, that sexuality is not inherently static and readily classifia-ble. In the face of this, fatness and bisexuality become spectres, signs of defect or incompleteness or immaturity to be feared and rejected. They become temporary categories which must be disciplined into maturity and coherence, lest the whole edifice fall apart.

Much of fat and bi activism emphasizes that fatness and bisexuality are mature, stable and coherent. They assert that they are "natural" states of being which are not chosen, and generally cannot be chosen. I must stress that this work is im-portant. This chapter is not meant, in any way, to devalue the fat and bi activists doing that work. Getting people to under-stand that diet culture and conversion therapies do not work as advertised and instead cause immeasurable suffering means asserting the fact that fatness and bisexuality exist and cannot be deleted through any amount of discipline (i.e. abuse). But I fear so much time is spent asserting the ways fatness mirrors thinness and bisexuals are similar to non-queer people that we risk missing the fundamental lie in thin/hetero logics. Within fat and bi politics is the potential to open up different ways of being which reject the Protestant Work Ethic and the capital-ism it underpins.

Fat politics asserts that fat people should be allowed to exist freely in the bodies we have now. Fat politics can also make the argument that, if we are unable to control what size our bodies will be, then performances of dietary virtue – through "proper" eating and exercise – become pointless. In such a framework, dietary virtue itself becomes meaningless; body size has noth-ing to do with (Anglo-American capitalist) "self-control", and everything to do with a blend of genetics, environment and random chance.

Thinness then, is not a marker of good moral character and has no philosophical meaning beyond that which is projected onto it. Rejecting food as pleasure does not guarantee thinness. So that rejection, and the diet culture it creates/sustains, be-comes pointless. By demanding that fat people be allowed to enjoy full lives today, rather than waiting for a thin future that will never come, fat politics can take the performative morality out of food and movement. The way we eat and how much we move cease to be fatphobic shorthand or sorted into a moral hierarchy to be packaged and sold to us.

Bi politics argues that people should not be bound by the way they experienced love and attraction in the past. Bi poli-tics asserts that, if ways of engaging in romantic/sexual inti-macy can vary and change across a lifetime, then insisting on the purity/primacy of one attraction over another is doomed to fail. The idea that someone is heterosexual and so will fol-low the script laid out by heteronormativity unless definitively proven otherwise is shown to be inherently flawed. As queer-ness – often understood as rigid homosexuality – cannot be easily recognized and kept at a distance, heterosexuality cannot be a safe/easy default presumption. Since experiencing apparently heterosexual desire does not inherently purge queerness, then conversion therapies and other forms of enforced heterosexuality are not the safeguards they claim to be. Bisexuality has the ability to bring queer ways of being into apparently heterosexual unions. This means that the idealized heteronormative life plan – (cis)gender segregation, marriage until death and the associated children – and the stable unit of production it generates, cannot be inherent or automatic, even within heterosexual-appearing partnerships.

In these ways, the rejection of pleasure – in food or desire – cannot reliably turn a fat or queer person into a thin or cishet one. To put it another way, eschewing "sin" cannot reliably produce "purity". Therefore, fat and bi politics invite us to embrace pleasure now. We can understand that food and inactivity and desire and sex are sources of pleasure, that pleasure is to be appreciated and enjoyed. Fat and bi politics understands that we should not reject our present selves in favour of (thin) futures or (hetero/homosexual) pasts.

In a society that uses past behaviours to create present assets which are projected into future products, embracing change, fluidity and unpredictability can be a site of resistance. Rejecting consumer capitalism, which binds us to discrete groupings to sell us "aspirational" lifestyles, requires the rejection of thinness and heteronormativity as inherent goods. Understanding that much of our lives is out of our control, that all we can do is experience it, opens up space to show solidarity for one another, as no way of being can be inherently superior to another.

Faced with this truth, we are invited to reject the lie of the Protestant Work Ethic and therefore the idea that the size of our bodies or shape of our desires can be markers of virtue. We can instead confront the ways that vast swathes of the world's population are cut off from pleasure, either through inaccessibility or punishment.

In a world which seeks to silo us, divide us between the deserving and the undeserving, turn power and privilege into moral superiority, make control over capital a sign of virtue, fat and bi politics has the potential to provide important ways of rejecting/resisting/dismantling these power structures.

References

Tsai, A.G. & Thomas, A.W. (2005). Systematic review: An evaluation of major commercial weight loss programs in the United States. *Annals of Internal Medicine*, 142(1), 56–66.

Further reading

Brownell, K.D. & Rodin, J. (1994). Medical, metabolic, and psychological effects of weight cycling. *Archives of Internal Medicine*, 154(12), 1325–1330.

Eisenberg, S. (2022). "10 examples of highly effective niche marketing strategies." Wrike, 16 June 2022. www.wrike.com/blog/niche-marketing-strategies.

"Fat acceptance movement." Wikipedia. https://en.wikipedia.org/wiki/Fat_acceptance_movement.

Ochs, R. (2020). "I call myself bisexual because..." Robyn Ochs, 9 October 2020. https://robynochs.com/2020/10/09/i-call-myself-bisexual-because.

"Protestant ethic." Encyclopedia Britannica. www.britannica.com/topic/Protestant-ethic.

CHAPTER 11

Staying Out of the Closet: Trans Intersectionality

Felix F Fern

Felix F. Fern (he/they) is an intersectional human rights activist, writer and public speaker whose work primarily focuses on transgender, sex worker and disabled people's rights in the UK. He is one of the co-founders of the grassroots organization Trans Activism UK.

At 13 years old, I mustered up the courage to have the dreaded "coming out" conversation with my mother. Sitting her down in the living room, I perched in the chair opposite her and announced, "I am transgender." She paused for a moment before asking, "Is that the one where you want to be a boy?" I nodded and then came the next part. "And I'm bisexual."

My mum's response was matter-of-fact. "So what do you want me to do about it?" Well, I was hardly expecting the Times Square New Year's ball drop, but I thought I'd get something! I'd paced outside the living room door for what felt like decades, my stomach churning. I'd spent hours reading stories of parents storming out of the room, melodramatic tears, and declarations of "I'll love you know matter what" as parents embraced their terrified children.

What I received, however, was apathy. Looking back, this shouldn't have come as much of a surprise to me as "apathy" is how you could have summed up the parenting style in my home as I was growing up, but I was filled to the brim with all of this pent-up energy that suddenly had nowhere to go.

There's a blessing and a curse that many autistic and neurodivergent people have, especially when you're young, where you have this amazing ability to just figure yourself out. I saw the word "transgender" online and my brain went, "Sweet, that's what that thing is that I'm experiencing. Sorted." There was no self-doubt, no intensive experimentation, just immediate acceptance and the start of a plan of what to do about it.

From a practical standpoint, it's definitely a time saver, but it can start to feel like a curse when you realize that the rest of the world doesn't just get on with it like you want to, and when they fail to accommodate what you think of as sensible plans. It becomes very frustrating very quickly.

So there I was, a young person using the internet as my guide to what you're supposed to do when you realize you're queer, and I'd just completed Step One: Tell A Parent. What's Step Two? Well, tell your friends, of course! I could take all of that energy still buzzing around inside my skull and put it to good use, by telling my closest school friends.

My sense of relief at figuring out what to do next was short-lived. I went to a school that was deemed one of the worst out of 200 in Essex in the national press, and I told my three closest friends that I was bisexual. (I didn't get on to the "trans" bit until a while later.) My mum's sense of apathy definitely didn't apply to this preteen bombshell I'd just catapulted into the classroom. Despite already experiencing intensive bullying, I was a very trusting child, which meant that one of those friends wasted no time in alerting as many people as she possibly could within the hour.

This was during Section 28, so saying I had a bad time would be quite an understatement. For the next few years, I couldn't even walk from one classroom to the next without some pre-pubescent, squeaky-voiced little dipshit or overly aggressive girl coming up to me and saying, "Aren't you worried about AIDS?" "How do you know you're bi if you've never had sex?" "Do you fancy me?" "You're going to Hell."

It's too traumatizing to re-live the details of just how severe the bullying became but, after undergoing a fair amount of therapy, I now view surviving that experience as an achievement, despite the scars that serve as a reminder of the ordeal. It never managed to silence me or drive me back into the closet, and it is undoubtedly one of the driving forces of my activism. I do not want any child to go through what I experienced.

As I got older, I found it easier to come out to people, not because their attitudes had changed but because my own had developed to a point where nothing could be worse than that trauma I had experienced, so who cares if someone doesn't understand or approve of who I am attracted to? I knew that their opinion meant little in the grand scheme of things, and it would not prevent me from living my life.

However, when it came to my being openly trans, things were a little different. We now live in a world where, if you're out in the open, it's difficult to avoid having your trans identity dominate your sense of self. Contrary to popular belief in certain groups, this isn't because trans people are somehow lacking in any way, but because our society is so fixated on trans people as a concept that it's virtually impossible to escape.

You can't even see a GP without your transition being brought up in some way. This is so common, we had to coin a term for it: "trans broken arm syndrome". Imagine going to a doctor because you're suffering from an awful ear infection and you end up trapped in a room awkwardly trying to explain that no, you're not a trans woman, and yes, testosterone really can make your voice break (to a *medical professional!*).

The pressure of constantly having to explain elements of my identity took a toll on me and it wasn't just because I was transgender. Medical professionals, even in gender care, make binary assumptions that you must be either gay or straight, and you find yourself lacking the energy to speak up and correct them. This began to affect how I expressed my sexuality, and I eventually found that I labelled myself as "gay" in an effort to make things easier. Part of me enjoyed the simplicity; I think that a lot of monosexual people are unaware of the overwhelming confusion that people express when you're not just attracted strictly to one gender, and I was spending less energy on explaining myself to people. So I say that I never went back into the closet but, in essence, I was changing myself to fit society's expectations instead of expecting society to change for the better, and that meant tucking away part of the truth of my sexuality.

Before I knew it, I was seeking that comfort elsewhere in my life, and by my late twenties I was working in an office where no one knew I was trans, this thing I had been so relentlessly open about virtually since I was a child. Because I was "gay", no one questioned my femininity as a man, except for the older and more privileged male staff members who would question my nail polish, avoid mentioning sports or look mildly uncomfortable if left alone with me. I had long hair but I wore a suit, I was soft-spoken but my title was "Mr". You cannot underestimate the power of people knowing your full name and title. I'd get misgendered at the corner shop but at work, there was no doubt that I was anything other than A Man™.

There were the odd moments when my heart would start

racing at the thought of being clocked, like making sure I didn't wear anything that showed my chest scars on "Dress Down Fridays", being cautious whenever childhoods were discussed, and trying to get out of the "guess who is who by their childhood photos" game someone suggested.

But otherwise, I just kind of sailed by under the radar, and for the first time, my life felt easy (other than, you know, worsening physical health and crippling depression). I wasn't constantly being questioned, no one felt entitled to pry into my private life on a daily basis, and I had a vague if uncertain sense of belonging.

That is, until I found out that the LGBTQ+ staff support network was looking for new committee members, and that something they were specifically lacking was someone to lead on trans issues such as staff policies and general wellbeing in the workplace. I was practically salivating at the chance to combine my love of boring administrative work and being a shameless queer in one voluntary role, and the potential to be an annoying busybody was irresistible.

Before long, I was organizing charity LGBTQ+ History Month events (tip: if you want office staff to attend anything, just say there's cake), putting up posters about notable figures in queer history, and handing out rainbow lanyards to staff.

My line manager was furious. He was the only person in the office who knew I was trans, on a purely need-to-know basis, to ensure that I was able to get time off for medical appointments. I wasn't being quietly gay any more, I was visible, increasingly so, and I was being called in to regular meetings about the way I dressed, or the posters I put up, or any other thing that he could think of to send a not-so-subtle message: "If you're not careful, they'll realize you're not like them."

I snapped. Transgender Day of Visibility was around the

corner. It was my duty as a staff support network committee member to mark the occasion, so mark it I did. Our office had our regular "stand up" meeting, every member of staff was gathered to one end of the room, and I was given the opportunity to speak.

"Today is Transgender Day of Visibility... I am speaking about this day to you all because you all know someone who is transgender, whether you're aware of it or not. You will have come across someone in your life who is trans, so these are not issues that don't impact you. They do impact you because they impact me, because you know me, and I am transgender."

I had never seen my manager's face go so red. I was called in for another meeting. Although my life at the office was never the same after that, I outlived the old guard of ageing white cisgender straight men holding positions of authority over me. In time, they were replaced by younger, more inclusive staff, including my own line manager who was replaced by someone who had done gender studies at university and made banging chocolate Welsh cakes.

While all of this was happening, trans issues in the government, the news and the mainstream media were becoming increasingly prominent. Theresa May's promise to reform the Gender Recognition Act to be more accessible and inclusive was nowhere to be seen, Graham Linehan was campaigning against Mermaids (a charity that supports families of trans children), and the Gender Critical movement was beginning to bloom. Signs of it among the odd older woman in the office were even beginning to take form (though, much like the rest of wider society, other staff did not stand for such behaviour).

Before too long, the pandemic hit and I found myself working from home. It was becoming difficult to extract myself from the worsening conditions for trans folks, and every spare second I had during work was spent reading the news and being filled with dread.

On Sunday 14 June 2020, I woke up to the news that *The Times* had published an article titled "Boris Johnson scraps plan to make gender change easier" (Shipman, 2020). My stomach sank. The one tiny sliver of hope that the Conservative government had given us, Theresa May's promise, was being taken away for good.

I logged into Facebook. I went to the "Events" tab, and I typed into the title bar: "Trans Rights Protest. 4 July, Parliament Square, London."

What the *fuck* was I doing?

Black Lives Matter protests had been popping up around the globe as a result of the tragic murder of George Floyd so at this point I had seen countless news stories, watched the video clips, and heard the chants. In my naivety, I found myself seeing these demonstrations and thinking, "How hard could it be?" But I had never been to a protest, let alone called for one! All I had was the Green and Black Cross website (still to this day an integral resource)[1] and a lot of desperation.

I didn't know any activists, I was miles from London, and we were in full lockdown (4 July was the first day that some hospitality and leisure venues would be reopening). I had zero knowledge or experience, I was just scared and angry and I couldn't sit around waiting for the next bad piece of news to come by without doing something, anything.

I still get emotional when I think about the day. My partner at the time drove me to London and dropped me off. I loitered

---

1   Green and Black Cross is an independant, grassroots organization which provides mutual aid and legal support to protesters in England and Wales. See website: greenandblackcross.org

awkwardly at the border of Parliament Square, a megaphone hanging off the side of my rollator. I was early to help prepare, but there were already people gathering.

The light blue vests of police liaison officers started gathering too, but they were outnumbered by the sea of flags that started to appear. If you can imagine a variety of queer pride flags, they were all there. It got to the point where police had to give in and allow people onto the grass because there simply wasn't enough room.

I went into full organizer mode, putting all of my attention into ensuring that speakers knew when they were up and that everyone was feeling safe and okay. I was supposed to give an opening speech but I just couldn't, I'd never done any public speaking and I was petrified and on the verge of hyperventilation.

Speaker, after speaker, after speaker. Clapping, laughing, crying. There was a massive roster of speakers, with a priority on Black and Indigenous people of colour (BIPOC) and intersectionality marginalized folks, and I could not believe just how smoothly things were going.

Finally, by the end of it, I felt confident enough to go up and speak, but that's when I realized that being at the front of a protest looking forwards, as well as being short and using mobility aids, means that you're not able to tell how many people have actually turned up. I got up onto the steps and only then did I find out that we had filled Parliament Square with over two thousand people, and as soon as I started speaking I had to stop.

"I could lose my job for being here" was one of the few things I remember saying. I was a civil servant, and what I was doing was prohibited, but it didn't matter. Every inch of my body was full of pride, and for the first time in my life I felt part of a community.

But how on earth did this happen? I definitely skipped a

few steps in this story, and that's because while this event was momentous and is something that I will never forget, hindsight is 20/20 and I learned a lot from that day.

We were far too gracious with the police; I allowed big personalities to almost completely ruin the entire organization of the day; I didn't know enough about genuine safety for marginalized communities; and while my style of protest organization results in a good show, it doesn't guarantee change.

There are two key takeaways both from that day and from the many other protests that I have organized since that I believe can be useful to everyone:

- Anyone can organize a protest. Even if you've never been to one, even if you're autistic, even if you're in a wheelchair, even if you're scared to talk to people.
- Everyone has their own individual strengths and you can bring that strength to activism, no matter what it is. Mine is administration (I don't know any other activists who run their protests with a spreadsheet), whereas the activists and groups that I collaborate with are strong in areas that I'm awful in.

The reason that day was so successful, despite its flaws, is because of the wider community. This was a very important issue and a lot of people were angry, and turning that anger into action is the foundation of activism, but you simply cannot do it alone.

I used my experience in administration to take on an organizational role, using application forms to get and sort speakers, writing template emails to invite people, and maintaining a spreadsheet to ensure that all information was accessible and could be obtained efficiently. By getting the word out via social media I was able to connect with people who had prior activism experience and knowledge. Without them, there would have been no protest.

Though we are small and humble, now I do everything through my team Trans Activism UK, a grassroots activism organization that focuses on trans equality in the UK but thrives in intersectionality. Both of the people I founded Trans Activism UK with are people I met that day in Parliament Square. We were all doing something for the first time, with me organizing the event, Shaira Choudhury speaking on the impact of colonialism and Amelia Decruz coming along to protest and support. We also wouldn't have got anywhere without the amazing support and hard work of Laura Kate Dale, who is an activist in her own right.

Now we have two years of several protests, open letters, online campaigns, media appearances, panels and so on under our belts, simply because we are ordinary people with ordinary strengths who care a great deal about trying to make things better.

Without this activism experience, I never would have been aware of the fact that there is an equally thriving, passionate and truly diverse bi+ activism movement in the UK that had been happening under my nose the whole time. Something I strongly stand by is the importance of intersectionality, and one of the wonderful benefits of it is that you're introduced to other communities that may already welcome you.

I have learned to be louder about every part of my identity through the practice of activism, and that is why I no longer tuck my bisexuality away in favour of simplicity. Instead, I embrace it with love for both myself and my multisexual spectrum community.

This has not only improved my own sense of self-worth and security in who I am, but it has also improved my activism. As Trans Activism UK, our primary focus is obvious, but we make a point to ensure that people have a platform to speak about every part of themselves, whether that's sexuality, disability, race, religion, life experiences and so on.

If you're going to stand up on a platform and shout about why you as a trans person deserve equal rights, you need to be able to take up space to let people know if that is not the only part of you that is in need of equality, that other groups you belong to are being failed by the government, the mainstream media and society as a whole.

I feel extremely privileged that the bi+ activism movement has accepted me and afforded me so many wonderful opportunities to discuss the issues that we face as bisexual and m-spec[2] individuals. It was through watching my fellow bi+ activists, work (through books, panels, speeches, etc.) that I realized how I had been holding back such a wonderful part of my identity for the sake of simplicity. How can I set an example as someone who boasts the importance of intersectionality if I cannot own all of the wonderful different elements that make me the person that I am?

I fight for trans equality, I fight for disability equality, I fight for sex worker equality, and I fight for bisexual equality.

Reference

Shipman, T. (2020). "Boris Johnson scraps plan to make gender change easier." *The Times*, 14 June 2020.

---

2   "M-spec" is short for "multiple-attraction spectrum" or "multisexual spectrum", an inclusive umbrella term for the many different ways people express attraction beyond gender. M-spec includes people who use words for themselves such as bi, pan, omni, fluid, flexible, curious, and more, as well as some people who don't use labels at all.

CHAPTER 12

A Quick Guide to the Experiences of Arrival and Settlement of LGBTQ+ Forced Migrants in the UK

Ourania Vamvaka-Tatsi

Ourania (Rania) Vamvaka-Tatsi (she/her) has been the key organizer for the LGBTQ+ PoC refugee and asylum-seeker community in Wales since 2016. She is the co-chair of Glitter Cymru and founder/chair of Glitter Sisters. Rania is in the final year of her PhD, which focuses on queer asylum policy, at the School of Social Sciences, Cardiff University. Rania is the co-convenor of GASP, a grassroots research group that focuses on progressing the academic and public discourse around gender and sexuality. Over the years, Rania has worked closely with various third-sector organizations and the Welsh Government on LGBTQ+ specific policies; most notably she is part of the expert panel of the recent LGBTQ+ Action Plan, and she led and researched Wales's first ever report on LGBTQ+ asylum-seeker housing needs. Currently, she works as the Policy & Research Lead for the biggest youth homeless charity in Wales.

Geographies of family history and privilege

I was born and raised in Athens, Greece; I am a bisexual woman of mixed heritage. I am not a refugee nor an asylum seeker in the UK, but I come from families with long histories of forced migration.

I came out as bisexual around the age of 17 years old. My parents did not know how to deal with it. As expected, they thought it was just a phase and ignored it. Back in the early noughties, in the European South, LGBTQ+ rights were unheard of. Bisexuality was understood as either an exclusively "girl thing" with the sole purpose of turning the threesome fantasies of cisgender, straight men into reality, or as a rite of passage to become a fully fledged lesbian. Bisexual erasure was alive and well.

I was getting increasingly frustrated having to constantly educate friends, family and partners on what being bisexual means to me. Their blatant ignorance, mixed in with the wonderful Greek machismo, forced me to experience various forms of emotional, physical and sexual violence. There was no LGBTQ+ community to stand by my side. All I wanted was to be able to be authentically myself, and for my sexuality not to be denied, devalued or fetisized.

This was one of the main reasons why I left Greece and migrated to the UK. Because of my lack of understanding of what an organized and cohesive LGBTQ+ community looks like and how it operates, it took me a while to get involved in any LGBTQ+ groups in Wales. Also, Wales in 2011 lacked safe, sober spaces that were exclusively for queer people of colour. In 2016, I joined Glitter Cymru, a grassroots organization based in Cardiff for LGBTQ+ people of colour and people from ethnically diverse backgrounds. Through Glitter Cymru, I became close friends with LGBTQ+ refugees and asylum seekers and my journey in activism began. Since my family's refugee experiences are so close to my heart, I wanted to use my research skills to amplify the voices, and highlight the unique issues faced by the LGBTQ+ forced migrants I met through Glitter Cymru. Seven years on I am the co-chair of this wonderful organization, leading on the LGBTQ+ forced migrant research and policy in Wales. Glitter is the first and only organization of its kind in Wales.

The life stories of refugees and asylum seekers need to be told, for those with privilege to understand the consequences of their political choices on a global scale. I am one of the lucky ones: I grew up listening to my grandparents narrating their memories of seeking refuge in Greece in the mid-1930s. Due to political and religious persecution, my family fled North Egypt, Southeast Turkey and South Albania. Some family members were grateful for the help they received along the way, but remained proud of their refugee background and celebrated their cultures through food and vibrant parties with their siblings and friends who survived the journey. Others were always secretive and purposefully vague about their journey. Both sides were forced to assimilate quickly, which started by being baptized Greek Orthodox and denouncing their native languages.

For years, these two different approaches to sharing and connecting with my family's refugee past had me thinking that there is a right and a wrong way of commemorating the hardships in your life. It took me years to realize how problematic that was. They didn't owe their stories to anyone, not even to close relatives, like me. Those stories were theirs and theirs alone. I should have felt privileged that they confided in me when they did; I should have felt privileged with the level of information and detail they shared or kept from me, as it was for them to decide. It was their choice to remember and their choice to forget. This is when I realized the power of identity erasure.

And I realized the power of celebrating refugee stories – stories that showcase the perseverance and resilience of the human spirit in the face of extreme adversity; stories that do not follow a linear path; asylum experiences that vary from traumatic to contradictory; stories that shape generations and the idea of "home", not as space but as a feeling of safety and intimacy.

In this chapter, I discuss some of the most significant barriers faced by LGBTQ+ forced migrants in the UK, with a special focus on Wales. I emphasize the lived experiences of discrimination resulting from immigration and asylum policies. I explore how bisexual refugees and asylum seekers experience otherness and I raise questions around ideas of belonging and acceptance. I am aware of the vast differences between LGBTQ+ expressions, but for the purpose of this chapter, I will be using the acronym as an umbrella term.

Brief background on UK migration policy

Over the years, refugees and asylum seekers have become symbols of displacement and global mobility. Their journeys are understood as disruptive and even when they reach a safe destination, local social structures impact their access to networks, damaging their community experiences. Such experiences are more difficult for LGBTQ+ people of particular ethnic groups. In migration policy, refugees and asylum seekers are defined through their status; refugees have successfully gone through the legal process of seeking asylum. Asylum seekers are still in that legal process, which can take from three months to ten years. During that process, their social rights are limited. For example, they cannot work, and they do not have access to education and private housing. The Home Office explains that the UK is the first option for asylum claims based on sexual orientation, particularly from people from former British colonies.

Colonialism, among other things, is responsible for imposing socio-economic and cultural systems that continue to have detrimental results for LGBTQ+ rights in post-colonial societies. Colonialism is also responsible for creating, implementing and spreading a set of legal codes that were prevalent throughout the colonies, especially from 1860 onwards, which criminalized homosexual conduct and punished it with long-term imprisonment and death. These violent legal codes became an integral part of the British colonies' legal system that was enforced throughout Africa and Asia. This legacy has influenced former British colonies' current national laws on LGBTQ rights around the world.

In 2012, the UK government introduced the Hostile Environment Policy, which is designed to make the UK a difficult place to live for people without a leave to remain, such as asylum seekers. In 1999, the Immigration and Asylum Act centralized housing and welfare assistance. The National Asylum Support Service (NASS) was created in 2000 to coordinate accommodation and financial support for asylum seekers. Under Section 4 of the 1999 Immigration and Asylum Act, asylum seekers have the option of a weekly allowance, which in 2023 stands at £49.18 per week, primarily chosen by those who already have family and friends in the UK. Under Section 95 of the Act, those who do not have any family or friends to stay with are provided with the weekly allowance, plus accommodation on a "no-choice" basis, which means being moved wherever accommodation is available. Through NASS, the Home Office has awarded the responsibility for asylum housing to private companies.

Quote from an LGBTQ+ forced migrant:
Back then my English was limited so when I claimed asylum I thought I was going to stay in London. To be honest with you, I wanted to stay in London because of the great gay scene. I agreed to come to Wales because I didn't realize how far from London it is, I actually thought Wales was a neighbourhood in London. I was very shocked when the driver told me Wales is another country! I had no choice but to come here.

Housing

When asylum seekers start their legal journey in the UK, housing is one of the first barriers they face. Most of the LGBTQ+ asylum seekers wish to stay in London because of its vibrant LGBTQ+ scene. This is rarely the case, and they are not given the option on where to live in the UK. This touches on the UK's policy of "no-choice displacement", which is designed to discourage asylum seekers from entering the UK and is associated with enhancing the stress of the asylum process. The "no-choice displacement" policy evokes loss of power, which is especially significant for the LGBTQ+ claimants who were exposed to human rights violations.

Quote from an LGBTQ+ forced migrant:
They asked me if I had any friends or family here that I can stay with. I don't. They then said that they could only offer accommodation in Wales – this was pretty much an ultimatum between Wales or being homeless, I guess.

NASS has dispersal areas all over the UK. On arrival in a dispersal area, the asylum seekers are directed to a hostel which is run by the Home Office. The hostels generally operate a sign-in/sign-out system, as they wish to keep track of occupants coming and going. The mealtimes are set, with an early dinner time. If asylum seekers miss a meal, they must wait for the next one. The hostel's management appears apathetic to socio-cultural differences, variances of religious beliefs, sexual orientation, and the gender identity of the residents. This results in incompatible residents being forced to co-exist in small rooms, with up to six beds. This lack of personal space and privacy often leads to tensions and violent outbursts. The LGBTQ+ asylum seekers are especially vulnerable. To protect themselves, they choose to not engage with their roommates and others in the hostels. They often describe the atmosphere at the hostel as toxic, dangerous and homophobic. LGBTQ+asylum seekers highlight that they feel unsafe and abused in the dispersal accommodation.

> **Quote from an LGBTQ+ forced migrant:**
> The House staff did not ask if I am comfortable with sharing a room. I was sleeping in a room with five men. That gave me serious anxiety and I was afraid to speak because I did not want people to know I am gay.

They often go "back in the closet" out of fear for their lives, which is detrimental to their mental health. They perform heteronormativity in order to protect themselves, as homophobia, transphobia and biphobia are additional pains. The hostel staff disregard racist incidents caused by ethnic-cultural and religious differences. LGBTQ+ asylum seekers are at higher risk of sexual harassment, non-contact violence and victimization in the hostels, especially if they do not pass as straight. Most LGBTQ+ asylum seekers are separated into rooms based on their country of origin. This creates further complications, as in many cases they are housed with the people they were trying to escape from. This often leads to loneliness, suicide attempts and post-traumatic stress.

> **Quote from an LGBTQ+ forced migrant:**
> There were a few more Afghan men at the House and I think they understood by my manners that I'm gay. Even though they never blatantly asked me if I'm gay, they were making homophobic jokes loudly outside my room so I can hear them, they were eyeing me up and down in the corridors, whispering abuse, or making sexual hand gestures. They refused to sit and eat with me like I have cholera or something. I was crying myself to sleep every night. I left Afghanistan to escape all of this. I came to the UK to be free and be myself. The moment I entered the House, I was back in the closet.

Long stays in the hostels are not unheard of. After 60 days or more of living at the hostel, the second phase of the asylum process begins, when they are moved into dispersal accommodation. The move to their new accommodation tends to be a violent transition, as they struggle to cope with their new surroundings. Private housing providers used by the Home Officer usually fall below acceptable standards of living, posing a significant risk of fire. The asylum seekers' bedrooms are small, with old, used furniture and metal bars at the windows to avoid further suicides. Such accommodation is found in areas of low housing demand that usually suffer from high levels of crime, low levels of tolerance towards the LGBTQ+ community and unwelcoming views on migration. As a result, the LGBTQ+ asylum seekers keep to themselves, locked in their rooms, isolated from any LGBTQ+ organizations that could help with their integration. As they do not want to be further harassed or assaulted in the dispersal accommodation, most of them do not engage with their housemates. Their mental health declines and many begin to self-harm.

Quote from an LGBTQ+ forced migrant:
I was just settling in the new house when the manager came and said, "On Monday you are moving to Swansea." That was on a Saturday morning. That is not even two days notice. I had no choice; you are not allowed to argue. That move knocked me down. I did not know anybody in Swansea. I had to start again from zero. It took me a long time to build up my mental health. For six months, I closed myself off, and I was not even getting out of the House. I was so alone.

Quote from an LGBTQ+ forced migrant:
The move increased my anxiety. I was embarrassed to bring friends over because the new house was a mess. My room was so small that when I stretched my arms I could almost touch both walls. The furniture was old and destroyed, the walls were dirty and full of holes and the carpet had stains. My room had only one window but it had bars so I don't jump out. Apparently, it happened a lot.

The asylum seekers remain in the dispersal accommodation for the duration of their claim. Their transition to a private tenancy, if their claim is successful, is problematic. Since they live off £49.18 per week and they are not allowed to have a bank account, it is very challenging to gather enough money for a deposit. Most of them do not have any local contacts to use as guarantors or references. Lots of new refugees end up being homeless. The lucky ones who have made local friends tend to stay with them until they get a job and can save money for a deposit. Many private landlords and estate agencies decline the applications of new refugees.

> **Quote from an LGBTQ+ forced migrant:**
> The new housemates were very indifferent. We just said "hi" and "bye" and that's about it. Which is totally fine by me, after what I went through. I rarely saw them; we all kept in our rooms. At least there I could close the door and be myself, in peace and quiet.

Authenticating sexual orientation

All asylum applications are dealt with through the New Asylum Model (NAM). Each asylum claim is allocated a single case owner who is responsible for each stage of the application process, from contacting the asylum seeker to conducting the interviews. The interview is one of the most important parts of the process, as during the interview the claimants explain the reasons why they are fleeing their home country, and argue why they deserve the refugee status. This is a lengthy process that often results in rejection, multiple court appeals or even involuntary deportation. The Home Office does not offer guidance on the asylum interviews. The applicants' mental health is severely affected by the lack of sensitivity around these interviews. The interview becomes even more stressful if the claimant is not proficient in English and requires a translator. There is a lot of discussion around the lack of accuracy of translation during the Home Office interviews. This is especially problematic for

LGBTQ+ claimants who may use colloquial words to describe their sexuality or gender identity that may not be understood by the translator and be skipped as unimportant or be mistranslated to make sense to the interviewer, instead of focusing on ensuring that the claimant's point is clear. According to the Home Office, the interview process is transparent, but they have made it clear that their purpose is to uncover illegitimate claims. This attitude is particularly problematic when relating to LGBTQ+ asylum seekers, who are called to justify the authenticity of their sexuality and gender identity by narrating in graphic detail their sexual experiences, giving examples of sexual violence, and to prove to the Home Office interviewer that their identity is not fraudulent.

> **Quote from an LGBTQ+ forced migrant:**
> I was allocated my asylum interview after a month. It was an awful interview. The guy was asking me unnecessary questions like "When did you find out you are gay? How did you know you are gay? When were you first sexually harassed? How were you sexually harassed?" I said to him, "How do these questions help? Why are they important?" and he said, "Because lots of people lie about their sexuality and if the Home Office does not believe you are gay, you are not gay." He was explicit. He told me he judged the way I look to make the decision, and he said, "You do not look too gay, you can be discreet in your country." He said that to my face. As I expected, I got rejected the first time. I was a mess when I found out. My court was a month later. That month I was emotionally suffering. My court appeal was successful, but it was horrible to be interrogated about my sex life in front of a judge.

As the LGBTQ+ claims are seen by the Home Office as more

complex, the claimants must produce concrete evidence of continuous activity in local LGBTQ+ community groups or establish evidence of a long-term same-sex partner. These requirements are not always met, due to reasons varying from being displaced in areas with no LGBTQ+ community structures, to internalized homophobia/biphobia and lack of sexual partners. As a result, the asylum seekers' power relies on the narrative of self-identity as their only evidence. Such a narrative is especially challenging for bisexual claimants and bisexual women with children. In most cases, bisexual forced migrants escape abusive forced marriages, and survive corrective gang rapes as well as trafficking. Proving validity of their bisexuality is a herculean task, especially when claimants are required to present a linear and coherent, well-constructed, well-narrated life story in a language that may not be their mother tongue. They are essentially obliged to re-live traumatic experiences, and in many cases to describe in detail persecution, trauma, sexual violence, assault and torture.

Quote from an LGBTQ+ forced migrant:

I had a panic attack as soon as I got back home because the interview brought back so many bad memories. I would rather not talk about what I experienced being gay back home. I understand that the Home Office has to find out if we are claiming asylum for the right reasons, but they should come up with less degrading questions.

The Home Office completely disregards that LGBTQ+ claimants often struggle with repression and denial. The decision-makers are expected to ask for intrusive clarifications, to "catch out" the fake LGBTQ+ claimants. The asylum seekers, who tend to distrust figures of authority because of the treatment they had in their home countries, usually do not want to share intimate details but they are aware that shying away or refusing to answer will be detrimental to their claim. Over the years, many LGBTQ+ claimants have developed various coping mechanisms to avoid stigmatization – "trying to pass" or perform heteronormativity by wearing clothes that will not be seen as queer, or adopting language, behaviours and lifestyles that are understood through a heteronormative lens. Therefore, disclosing and openly discussing their sexual orientation is understandably threatening and uncomfortable, especially for those who come from societies with oppressive regimes or anti-LGBTQ+ legislation.

> **Quote from an LGBTQ+ forced migrant:**
> I told him as much as I could remember but he was persistent and it was like he was trying to test if he can catch me lying. I have been through so much and I've buried most details of my life so I can move on. I saw a couple of my gay friends being beaten up and dragged through the streets of my town. I'm sorry if I don't remember who I fucked in March or April 2007.

The success of the claim rests heavily on the Home Office interviewer's knowledge of new debates around sexuality and gender orientation. The interviewer's interaction with the asylum seeker, who is not in a position of power, is paramount. The interviewer chooses how to make the asylum seeker feel about their sexual identity in that moment, what information they regard as necessary for the claim and how they choose to extract it. This means that all LGBTQ+ asylum narratives are not negotiated through the claimants' self-identification but are assessed against whether they fit within the Western notions of sexual orientation and gender identity. This is a deeply essentialist perspective, as the claimants' self-identification is solely understood through a particular Western socio-cultural lens. This white supremacist lens erases people of colour from the LGBTQ+ spectrum, and their unique gender identities and sexuality expressions are not perceived as queer but as "foreign" and "exotic".

> **Quote from an LGBTQ+ forced migrant:**
> I was trying to be somebody else. I was trying to be straight to please my mum, my dad and the family and for a bit I thought I was over it – that it passed and I wasn't bi anymore. But then I'd see an ex of mine on the street and I'd ran home and not leave my room for days or weeks. How could I possibly have explained to a white, British, straight Home Office dude that I hated myself, I hated being bi every single day of my life?

Ultimately, this dictates that sexuality for the Home Office is strictly binary – either straight or gay – and inflexible, rejecting diverse transgender identities and erasing bisexuality, as it is understood as non-concrete and even fake. This results in more and more cases of LGBTQ+ asylum seekers playing up to the white supremacist stereotypes of gender and sexuality. They perform male gay expression as exclusively fem, bisexuals self-erase their sexuality to be categorized as lesbians or gay, and fem lesbians fine tune the "stone butch" look and attitude. This essentialist point of view indicates that the Home Office considers only binary, Westernized LGBTQ+ identities as authentic and awaiting to be discovered by the decision-maker, regardless of the claimant's real expression. This argument presupposes that the queer identity is white. If the queer person is a person of colour, their queerness must be justified and seen to be believed and packaged in a way that is palatable to the decision-maker. Thus, the Home Office interviews assume that all claimants share the same experiences and identity, disregarding the fact that sexual and gender identities can change over time and are socio-culturally specific.

Othering

The experiences of "othering" are initiated by the Home Office's obstructive settlement process. The lack of signposting to relevant, local LGBTQ+ organizations and support services is detrimental to community-building for those who need it the most. In fact, the community needs of LGBTQ+ asylum seekers and refugees are completely ignored by the Home Office. If they are lucky, they are signposted to organizations that run generic programmes for forced migrants, thus completely disrespecting the intersectional identities of LGBTQ+ forced migrants. Unfortunately, their specific life experiences make them "others" in both the local LGBTQ+ community as well as the forced migrant community. Their struggles are not fully understood by either community.

> **Quote from an LGBTQ+ forced migrant:**
> People who say that Wales is diverse are clearly blind and do not live in the real world. I'm a gay refugee from Tunisia – I'm a minority within a minority – within a minority! It's almost impossible to find people like me around here because Cardiff is so small! The gays here are visible but they are not very welcoming and they don't socialize with ethnic minorities, because they don't take us seriously. They have a very strong community; they do great art and charity events but they rarely invite people outside their circle, and when they finally do it costs money, which I don't have any. And don't get me started with

the refugees! They are so negative, all they do is complain that they can't find girlfriends, smoke shisha and talk about sports! I can't hang out with them, we are from different universes.

When the LGBTQ+ forced migrants attempt to socialize in the local LGBTQ+ community, if it exists, they are branded based on race, and they are seen either as "exotic" – indicating that whiteness is a prerequisite for membership in the community – or as "victims" that require saving. In both cases, they are othered and infantilized. These narratives of othering are particularly prevalent when the LGBTQ+ forced migrants are dispersed in areas of minimal diversity and tight socio-communal relationships that resist outside interference.

Quote from an LGBTQ+ forced migrant:
When I arrived I didn't know any other gay refugees. The refugees I knew were straight and I wasn't going to mix with them because they were homophobic, making jokes about "killing the gays". I wanted to meet people like me, who have gone through similar situations and will understand my struggles. I met a lot of Welsh gays at the clubs but nobody I could call a "friend". The club gays are white and I'm tall and black and I stand out. They think I'm "exotic" and entertaining because of my accent. At the club they smile and chat and they are friendly, but outside the club I'm just another foreigner on the street.

"Otherness" is a measure which allows or declines categorization; in the case of LGBTQ+ asylum seekers who are refugees, their racial, legal and socio-cultural otherness prohibits them from living as their authentic selves for the first time. LGBTQ+ forced migrants rarely start a romantic relationship in the UK, as they are seen by the local LGBTQ+ communities as "just for casual sex". Their emotional wealth is rejected based on their legal status. It is not rare for LGBTQ+ forced migrants to receive hate speech and further discrimination when using dating apps. This rejection from the local LGBTQ+ communities suggests that there is a very tangible fragility within the LGBTQ+ community that is undercut by lack of understanding and appreciation of the complexity of LGBTQ+ experiences that are "outside the norm". This fragility in less diverse communities highlights the tensions that are triggered by newcomers and questions the pre-established homogeneity, attitudes and behaviours of these communities.

> **Quote from an LGBTQ+ forced migrant:**
> Because of the way I dress people always shout abuse on the street, or they throw things at me but I'm not going to hide myself. When I moved to the UK I hoped to find a place where I can be myself but it turns out I don't fit in in the ethnic minorities' neighbourhood because I'm gay and I'm not super welcomed by the LGBTQ community because I'm a brown refugee. I really don't know where is my place in this world.

When the forced migrants attempt to celebrate their identities in LGBTQ+ clubs and bars they face further obstacles. Most of the time the bouncers do not allow them to enter, as they do not see their green ID card provided by the Home Office as legitimate, causing further socio-legal othering. For many, going to an LGBTQ+ only venue is a dream of a lifetime, but they are forced to distance themselves from those venues. Slowly, the LGBTQ+ forced migrants face immovable cultural barriers within the local LGBTQ+ community, which yet again, forces them to negotiate their otherness through negative behaviours and offensive attitudes.

> **Quote from an LGBTQ+ forced migrant:**
> You know I never had a boyfriend in Wales? I dated a few people but I got super tired because it was the same story again and again. At first, they were all curious to date a brown fem but then they treat me like their humanitarian deed of the month! This one guy insisted that I met his friends only after four dates. He introduced and they were like, "So you are the HIV positive refugee from Tunisia!" Who says that! I felt like one of those circus people in the Victorian times, like an exhibit for them to look at and comment on. I was so humiliated. I left early and never saw the guy again.

Conclusion

Through researching the lived experiences of LGBTQ+ forced migrants, one thing has become clear: it is paramount to further highlight the nuances relating to the lives of bisexual forced migrants. Currently, there is very little evidence specifically on their experiences and unless the researcher is aware of issues such as bi-erasure, the valuable voices and stories of bisexual asylum survivors get overlooked or, worse, lost.

The LGBTQ+ forced migrant experiences are precarious; their identities are negotiated through a restrictive immigration system that does not welcome them, nor does it offer opportunities for community building. They are treated as unwanted, as a burden and they are left to their own devices to navigate a vastly different socio-cultural and political landscape.

LGBTQ+ forced migrants have to deal with essentialist policies and practices that reduce their life narratives to harmful stereotypes that lead to self-erasure and post-traumatic stress. The NASS services function within neo-colonial parameters and reject the specific requirements of such a marginalized population. LGBTQ+ refugees and asylum seekers are forced to disclose intimate details regarding their sexual orientation and re-live and narrate traumatic experiences of violence. Protecting the mental health of LGBTQ+ refugees and asylum seekers during their resettlement process should be a governmental priority, instead of further damaging them.

The Home Office's systematic presentation of LGBTQ+ asylum seekers and refugees as untrustworthy and inauthentic claimants highlights a violent scrutiny of the LGBTQ+ expression and identities. Such Home Office processes are underpinned by narratives of homophobia, transphobia, biphobia and racism, thus demonstrating deep, systemic ignorance.

It is paramount to highlight that further research is required to examine the nuances of the experiences of bisexual forced migrants in the UK, and the specific approaches taken by bisexual activists to highlight such marginalized voices.

As the LGBTQ+ asylum seekers and refugees are forced to exist within particular social boundaries and are defined by their legal status and ethnic backgrounds, their lived experiences reflect a lack of social inclusivity and questions around belonging. LGBTQ+ forced migrants negotiate their own identities through new community memberships, far away from home, and the very least we can do is act as a true sanctuary and embrace them.

CHAPTER 13

Why I Call Myself Anarchabisexual

Shiri Eisner

Shiri Eisner (they/them) is a bisexual, genderqueer, feminist, and Mizrahi activist and writer living in occupied Palestine. They are the founder of (now defunct) anarchabisexual group Panorama – Bi and Pansexual Feminist Community, and the author of the book Bi: Notes for a Bisexual Revolution. *Most of their English-language writing is currently on X (formerly known as Twitter), where they can be found under @ShiriEisner.*

This text is dedicated to my late friend and partner Danielle DanVeg Sigawi (1991–2016), the only other person I knew who identified as anarchabisexual. May her memory be a revolution.

I have a tattoo on my forearm: my first, and seven years old at the time of this writing. It shows an anarchist "A" circled by a heart, with the inner part painted solid black. On its outer end, the heart branches down to create the (anarcha) feminist venus symbol, and upwards to the sides to create the transgender symbol (along with the venus symbol). It is overlayed with watercolor-style bi colour smudges. This tattoo stands for the core of my politics – the core of my heart and passion. My life-blood. This is my anarchabisexuality – and what this chapter is about.

Anarchism

It's difficult to speak with much capital-A "Authority" about anarchism. The boundaries of anarchism are difficult to chart. By its very nature, anarchism shuns singularity and authority. It is a creation of communal collaboration, an aggregate of knowledge and ideas that doesn't belong to anyone in particular, and (much like bisexuality) bends to no singular attempt to define and confine it. This is to say that in this chapter, I'll be sharing my own ideas and understandings of anarchism. However, nothing written about it can ever be definitive.

Anarchism is about resistance to any and all oppressive hierarchies, while recognizing intersections, as well as connections and parallels, between different struggles. This includes support of feminism, bi, queer and trans liberation, disability justice, decolonization, racial justice, ecological justice, animal liberation, and much more. This stems from an understanding that different types of oppression do not just intersect in the lives of people who belong to multiple marginalized groups. Rather, oppression against various groups bears a "family resemblance" – it works in similar ways and through similar (often the same) systems. In this way, anarchism's most basic position also provides the most solid and comprehensive basis the political landscape has to offer – the eradication of all oppression, with no caveats and no exclusions.

As opposed to most other social movements, anarchism recognizes capitalism and government as the two most comprehensive forms of control that perpetuate oppression in our lives. Capitalism is responsible for many effects of oppression that are often transparent and normalized (isolation, selling most of our lives to be able to survive, or equating labour with the value of human life, just to name a few). The government, on the other hand, has an exclusive licence to apply violence, with which it enforces the rule of capitalism. It utilizes this power through its police and military forces, prisons and various branches of government.

The goal of anarchism is to topple all forms of coercive control, to create a world that shuns structural power over others. For this reason, anarchism is also about hope. Most social movements confine their vision to the pragmatic – inserting a few corrections to the system without fundamentally changing it. In contrast, anarchists offer a comprehensive re-imagining of the world: recognizing all current forms of oppression while believing that we can be better, and do better. This means that when humanity charts its paths, these should never be limited to the constrained options set before us by dominant powers, but rather go far, far, beyond them – to a world where everyone can thrive.

But far from being utopian or focused on a distant intangible future, anarchism is also about praxis in everyday life. It is a "living force", expressed through direct action to tangibly improve our lives and the lives of our communities. This means both bringing resources directly to the people who need them, and resisting power directly where it is most harmful. And so, anarchism is also about mutual aid. Knowing that no one can save us but ourselves, and that that is a good thing. Knowing that, in response to capitalist alienation and hyper-individualism, loving each other, forming community, and giving each other practical help is a form of resistance.

Anarchafeminism

Anarchafeminism is the understanding that capitalism and government are patriarchal structures, and that patriarchy is upheld by capital and government. It's also the understanding that oppression doesn't only happen outside the home, but also in our personal lives. Traditionally – that is to say, in a way traditional for a movement created by men – the main sites for anarchist resistance are the workplace or the streets. But delegating politics to the public sphere, while maintaining that the private sphere – the home – is a haven blessedly free of societal oppression, is a staple of the patriarchy.

Thus, anarchafeminism is also about bringing politics into the private sphere, resisting oppression in our personal lives. It means recognizing the way in which cis men's control of capital within the family – literally the fact that they are considered the "owners" of the family, its finances and resources – also translates into power over others. This power forms a web that, together with other factors, spreads into control and violence, whether that be financial, emotional, physical or sexual.

For anarchafeminists, this also means being aware of patriarchal dynamics within the anarchist movement – from the privileging of (white cishet) men's issues, through who gets listened to in meetings, to who takes care of logistical tasks, and who does the so-called "glamorous" work. As a famous slogan goes, "the revolution begins in the sink".

Anarchafeminism is also about the understanding that feminism itself is incomplete at best and oppressive at worst if it doesn't also address other types of oppression. From the very inception of anarchafeminism in the early 20th century, anarchafeminist writers have been adamant that women's liberation is impossible so long as it preserves capitalist and state oppression. At best, it's a fight for scraps, and at worst, a fight for "equal access to exploitation". As Peggy Kornegger famously wrote in 1975, "Feminism does not mean female corporate power or a woman president: it means no corporate power and no president."

One more staple of anarchafeminism is the idea that none of us are free until all of us are free. This reflects the idea that various types of oppression are intrinsically linked, and that in order to be truly effective in our struggle for liberation, we have to include all other types of oppression within it. In addition, we aren't only fighting in solidarity with other groups, rather, we understand that oppression works in multiple, intersecting ways. That the link is not just theoretical, but also tangible in our lives.

Queer anarchism

Like its namesake queer, *queer* anarchism eludes definition. It is an expanse of meaning. It is rebellion in its purest form. It stands against everything and for everyone. It is "the cohesion of everything in conflict with the heterosexual capitalist world" and "a total rejection of the regime of the Normal" (Mary Nardini Gang, 2014). To be a queer anarchist is to be at odds with everything and yet to keep findings ways to relate to one another, create strange intimacies illegible to the cishet world, and struggle to free ourselves and each other from its clutches, from the clutches of everything standing to annihilate us (the deviants).

For me, queer anarchism is home – and the purest form of anarchism, because it doesn't fuck around (or, arguably, because it does *nothing but* fuck around). Queer anarchism meets us where we are, looks us in the eye and takes our hand to join the revolution. It shows us the way to do what we can, and that what we can do is a lot. It puts anarchism into our lives, making our lives into an anarchy, bringing our queerness, our strangeness, our oddity and lawlessness out into the world, and watching it all burn as we dance over the ruins. Queer anarchism is love, and it is hate, it is rage and hostility, and the wish to destroy everything and remake it into a world beyond our wildest dreams (and be assured, our dreams are wild).

Queer anarchism is the only form of anarchism that incorporates actual opposition to multiple forms of hierarchy and domination, rather than simply acknowledging them. Being the most intersectional and inclusive form of anarchism, it leaves almost no issue or group behind (almost – we'll get back to that later). It is the only undercurrent in anarchism that explicitly recognizes and acts in practice against multiple forms of oppression. And as opposed to intersectional queer activism, it doesn't stop at the boundaries of identity groups and -isms, but rather spreads its solidarity as broadly as possible, and focuses its analysis on systems, not biases. Nor does it seek to "normalize" queerness and assimilate into cishet patriarchal society. Instead, as befitting an anarchist ideology, it recognizes a myriad of powers, including capitalism and government, as sources of oppression and domination in our lives and the lives of others – and seeks to annihilate them.

As such, queer anarchists oppose LGBTQ struggles that mean to give us "a place at the table", or "a piece of the pie". This includes struggles around marriage, military service, reproduction or the procurement of children, rainbow capitalism, or increased police surveillance. As Kuwasi Balagoon (2019) wrote: "When a gay group protests lack of police protection, by making an alliance with police to form a gay task force, they ain't making a stand against the system, they are joining it." The same goes for all other entreatments to assimilate into the existing order. Instead of begging to be made part of the systems that are killing us, queer anarchists seek to overthrow them.

In terms of practice – if anarchafeminism brought politics into the private sphere, queer anarchism has brought the so-called "private" sphere out in public. This has very little to do with the liberal concept of "coming out", and everything to do with impropriety as oppressive society views it. Cishet patriarchy uses the constructs of privacy and propriety to keep us perverts and deviants away from the public sphere. We can see this every day now with the rising anti-LGBTQ and transphobic discourse, which asserts that our very existence is an improper disclosure at best, and a sexualized assault on children at worst. They imagine our lives as inherently subversive of public decency, requiring urgent removal from society.

Instead of trying to deny and placate, queer anarchists say yes to the horror that society harbours towards us. The Mary Nardini Gang (2009) writes:

> This culture has rendered us criminal, and of course, in turn, we've committed our lives to crime. In the criminalization of our pleasures, we've found the pleasure to be had in crime! In being outlawed for who we are, we've discovered that we are indeed fucking outlaws!

This means taking all the abject horror that society attributes to us, embracing it, and using it to fuel our rebellion and destroy society. Does that sound violent? It should. We harbour the annihilation of society as we know it. If they say we're dangerous – then yes, we are dangerous. If they say we represent chaos – then yes, we are chaos. If they say society should not be made to tolerate us – then we refuse to tolerate society.

This also means that queer anarchist tradition is full of trolling, parodying and humour. We reflect the caricature that society makes of us, and turn it back against it. Our goal is always to elude meaning, escape definition, and stretch the boundaries of the acceptable. One time, the Israeli anarchist queer group Mashpritzot organized a protest against public cisheterosexuality. Another time, they distributed pamphlets near a high school telling kids how to stop being cishet and become queer. San Francisco's Gay Shame have been known to burn pride flags in protest of assimilationism and capitalist pinkwashing. We are nothing if not provocative, and our provocation is all about taking public space and making it radically, anarchically, queer.

Queer anarchism is about refusing to play according to society's rules, and deliberately breaking them to make space for us – in all our magnificence, weirdness, wonder and monstrosity.

Except...

Opposing capitalism, government and hierarchy is not the only thing shared by all strains of anarchism. As any other movement that exists in an oppressive society, anarchism is, too, haunted by the very hierarchies it attempts to resist. I've already touched earlier on misogyny in anarchist movements. One might also add to this list ableism and transphobia (notably within the anarcho-primitivist strain, which advocates for an abandonment of technology and a return to "nature"). But the two most prominent forms of oppression that I have felt in the movement (as a disabled genderqueer bisexual person of colour, who is perceived as a woman) are racism and biphobia.

The anarchist movement is overwhelmingly white. This is a complicated issue, since most anarchists are honestly committed to fighting racism, colonialism and white supremacy. That is, of course, excluding *manarchists* – a name for anarchists (usually white cishet men) who feel that any struggle other than class struggle is a distraction from the "real" revolution. When engaging with anarchist communities, it is incredibly common to encounter white people of both these kinds. In fact, and unfortunately, unless an anarchist space is explicitly intended for people of colour, one can often find oneself being the only person of colour in the room. To add to that, a lot of the time, even the well-meaning white people end up centring themselves and taking over discussions.

But as a bi person of colour, I can say that at least they acknowledge that this is a problem. At least people of colour are largely recognized as valuable for the movement, and at least we have an anarchist people of colour movement. But you know what isn't acknowledged, almost ever? You guessed it, bisexuality.

All strains of the anarchist movement, including anarchafeminism and queer anarchism, are deeply committed to bi erasure and biphobia. Not monosexism, mind you. They're fine with attraction to more than one gender, just as long as it's not named as bisexual. And of course, the most intentional and informed commitment to biphobia comes from queer anarchism, as is traditional in queer communities.[1] This is particularly disturbing, because the queer anarchist movement is so intersectional, so good about connecting the dots of oppression, and because of its scathing criticism of nearly all other aspects of mainstream gay politics. In a movement where no stone is left unturned, the veritable boulder of biphobia is kept firmly in place.

---

1   Note that this doesn't make queer biphobia "worse". It's not the queers that are killing us, it's cishet society.

Most queer anarchist communities draw their views on bisexuality from the same old well, thoroughly explored in bi politics and theory: the idea that bisexuality is boring, non-political, non-subversive, reinforces the gender binary, is a privileged and oppressive identity, and many more similar notions. And perhaps this is why, despite copious queer anarchist cultural production (including books, articles, zines, blogs, posts, posters, pamphlets, actions, and more), only a handful of English-language texts have ever been published about anarchism and bisexuality.[2]

And perhaps this is the first reason why I call myself anarchabisexual – to make bisexuality present within anarchism (and anarchism present within bisexuality); to create a disruption, insist on making space where none is there. In the tradition of queer anarchism, it is about rage, resistance and solidarity. It's about taking what is forbidden and making it ours. It's about embodying the impossible, embracing everything imagined as wrong, and using it as a weapon against our oppression.

Anarchabisexuality is an ill-begotten monster born of two things that were never meant to exist: anarchism and bisexuality. And we are here to ruin everything.

Anarchist bisexuality

Despite all assertions about bisexuality's lack of relevance to liberation and resistance, in fact it harbours enormous subversive power against oppressive structures. The easiest way to find these

---

2   And out of these, only two have explicitly discussed the connection between bisexuality and anarchism: "Towards a Rational Bisexuality" (1971) and "The Fine Art of Labeling: The Convergence of Anarchism, Feminism, and Bisexuality" (1991).

powers is through the meanings that society gives bisexuality – and those are easily detectable through biphobic stereotypes.

The stereotypes tell us what dominant ideology "thinks" about bisexuality, the kinds of meanings that it attributes to it – and therefore the power it bestows on it. The stereotypes clearly reveal the ways in which society is afraid of bisexuality, and the damage that it can do to the cishet-patriarchal structure (and more).

In my book Bi: *Notes for a Bisexual Revolution* (Eisner, 2013), I collected a list of common stereotypes that reveal bisexualty's subversive power. Here they are.

Bisexuality doesn't exist

This is perhaps the most widely held belief about bisexuality. Society tells us that there is no such thing, and that those who claim to be bisexual are just wrong or misguided. This represents a wish that bisexuality didn't actually exist, an attempt to symbolically eradicate our existence. This is because bisexuality renders many oppressive systems inoperable. If it was truly recognized and incorporated by the dominant ideology, bisexuality would destroy the logic of cishet-patriarchy. The attempt to eliminate bisexuality's existence is an attempt to eliminate the subversive potential that it holds.

They say we don't exist – we say you don't want us to exist because we scare you. Our existence eradicates the foundations of your oppressive society, uproots the operating logic of your systems. Of course you want us gone – we destroy everything that you hold dear.

Bi people are confused, indecisive, or "going through a phase"

This stereotype is a "natural" extension of the first one, and it provides an elaboration on why bisexuality still doesn't exist, even though many people identify as bisexual. It imagines bisexuality as temporary, transitory, liminal and evasive. It means every manifestation of bisexuality is "not actually real" because it's transient. It imagines us as unstable, inconsistent and in constant doubt, alternating partners, genders and identities. So, in addition to trying to neutralize bisexuality's power in general, this stereotype specifically reveals society's fear of destabilizing the sexual and gender binary. It shows our power as destabilizing agents of chaos, promoting doubt in every oppressive structure.

They say we are confused – we say we delight in confusing you. We will break down your barriers, your divisions of inhumanity. We will inhabit your in-between, your impossibility, we'll confuse and confound your order, your social boundaries, and from the cracks where you placed us, we will break down your world.

Bi people are slutty, promiscuous, or inherently unfaithful

This one imagines bisexuality as excessive – and excessively sexual. Society is terrified of sex that isn't regulated and policed by the propriety of monogamous cishet-patriarchy. According to this stereotype, because bi people are attracted to more than one gender, we must be indiscriminate about our choice of partners. This makes us slutty, promiscuous, licentious, salacious. Delicious.

They say we're slutty – we say hell yes. We're sexual sluts, cuddle sluts and political sluts who will sleep and cuddle and bond with anyone because of their humanity and not their prescribed categories. Because of their magnificence and not their compliance. Outside the rigid rules that have policed, dictated and mutilated our lives. We recognize the pleasure in our bodies and the solidarity to be shared when we share our pleasure.

We want luxurious lushness for everyone, and we want to shape society as a form of indiscriminate pleasure. We claim pleasure as women, as trans and non-binary people, as asexual and aromantic, as disabled and chronically ill, as people of colour. We claim the pleasure that the world forbids us, and use it to power our resistance and liberate each other.

Bi people are carriers or vectors of HIV and other sexually transmitted infections

Relying on the previous stereotype, this one imagines bi people – and especially bi men of colour – as contagious vectors of disease, having unprotected bisex only to return home and infect their imagined innocent, cishet (often white) wives and children. This stereotype shows us society's fear of queer sexuality, as well as its ableism and the idea that disease and death are punishment for impropriety. AIDS, in particular, is imagined as the "queer disease", both a "punishment" for being queer and an embodiment of the cishet fear of being "infected" by queerness.

They say we're infectious – we say hell yes. You're afraid you'll catch our queerness, like a virus – we say we are the virus spreading through your system, taking root and destroying it from inside. We're a safety hazard for your monogamous, white, cishet bourgeoisie morals, and you cannot keep us out. You see our dark skins and fear for your whiteness – we say your white purity separates you from humanity, and we reach with loving arms to taint you, deface you and tear down your white supremacy. You see us and fear death – we say we are the death of your able-bodied order, and invade it with our beautiful, broken, magnificent, malfunctioning, marvellous, twisted bodies, our sick, brilliant, shattered, glorious minds. You are never safe from us. And like a virus, you will never see us coming until it is too late.

Bi people are actually gay or actually straight

This one tells us that bi people are anything other than bisexual. In addition to being an attempt to mutually exclude "gay" and "straight", it also reveals another assumption underneath: that bi women are "actually straight", while bisexual men are "actually gay". This shows us how society is projecting its own male-centrism by assuming that we are all really just into men – an assumption that itself relies on the notion that all penis-havers are men, and that all men have penises.

They say our lives revolve around penises – we say castrate society and its obsession with them. We contain multitudes, and we reject your coercive categories of gender and power based on genitals. Some of us have penises, some of us sleep with those who have them, and all of us reject the weight that you have placed on them. You say femme people are worthless and project your misogyny and transmisogyny on us – we embrace our wonderful trans selves, our bodies in all their glory, and spit in the face of your cishet-patriarchal order.

Bi people can choose to be gay or straight

This stereotype tries to again reduce us to monosexual categories, and does it while delegitimizing choice. In the battle between "gay" and "straight", both parties imagine that if anyone had a choice, they would always choose to be cishet. And more than that, they imagine choice itself as unnatural, inauthentic and illegitimate.

You say we have no place because we are unnatural – we say we stretch our imaginations to their limits and explore ways of life that your tiny world cannot imagine. We fill the world with opportunity and show you all the ways to free yourselves. You say we're unacceptable because we choose to live the way we do, and we say – you should join us. We've escaped your world into something better. Our worlds are expansive, our lives overflow with delicious possibility. We brim with the unimaginable, the possible and the impossible: we become everything we can be and everything we can't.

Bisexual anarchism

It's not just bisexuality that can parallel and draw from anarchism. Rather, they hearken to each other. Anarchism, in itself, parallels bisexuality in several ways that can help inform both politics and praxis.

As mentioned at the beginning of this chapter, both anarchism and bisexuality can never fully be defined. Their edges are fuzzy, and it's difficult to pick one singular definition for either of them. In fact, both their definitions are hotly contested in discourse and communities. Both anarchism and bisexuality have as many definitions as there are anarchists or bi people. Both represent an expanse that can be defined in a multitude of ways, and by its very existence, can blur boundaries and call other definitions into question. Their non-binary nature also means that they blur hierarchical distinctions and power structures – just what anarchabisexuality seeks to do.

It then follows that both anarchism and bisexuality are erased and denied for this very reason. Just like bisexuality, anarchism is systematically erased because of the threat that it poses against dominant ideology. They are erased both as a name and as a practice. If it does receive cultural attention, its presence is circumscribed, or presented as inherently negative and immoral. Just as bisexuality is often used to characterize villains, so is anarchism used to do the same. Anarchist rhetoric is often placed in the mouths of terrorists and other characters posing an existential threat to society.

Anarchism is also left unmarked when anarchist activists

participate in other movements, much like the way movements view bi activists (especially with regards to the LGBTQ movement). Both anarchist and bisexual activists have provided – and still provide – activist labour, effort and resources in a multitude of liberation and social justice movements. Sometimes they even create entire platforms on which movements can work (e.g. like bi activist Brenda Howard, who organized the first Pride march, and created the concept of Pride Week). Despite all this work and effort, those movements themselves often not only fail to acknowledge this, but also explicitly shun anarchism or bisexuality in general.

These similarities between bisexuality and anarchism mean that they share similar modes of operation within power. The threat that they both pose to oppressive social structures is already synchronized, and can be joined to create something both powerful and beautiful. They can meld together and create an explosion that would burn society like fireworks.

Anarchabisexuality in action

But anarchabisexuality is far from being just a form of political thought. It is also praxis, a mode of operation for our movements and activism.

Though there may have been other anarchist bisexual groups in other times and places, I am only familiar with two: Panorama in Tel Aviv (2008–2013), and the London Bi Pandas in London (2019–2020). Both groups serve as examples and inspiration for this type of political action, as well as provide lessons to learn from.

Panorama
Panorama – Bi and Pansexual Feminist Community was the

second bisexual organization in Israel/occupied Palestine. I started it because at the time, no bisexual community existed as such, nor any activism. In our years of activity, we formed a bisexual community that persists to this very day, and brought bi politics into both anarchist queer and mainstream LGBTQ discourses.

We first gained attention within the community following one direct action: after no bi representation was secured on stage at the 2009 Jerusalem Pride March, we jumped the fence and made our way backstage. While we were beaten and detained by security, one of us (Lilach Ben David) managed to get up on stage and speak about biphobia and bisexual erasure in front of the massive crowd. This was a seminal moment in the history of local bi activism, and it was followed by controversy for a full two months afterwards. It is also remembered as the one time in the history of the movement in Israel/occupied Palestine in which an LGBTQ organization used physical violence against activists from within the community.

Most of our activism concentrated on community building, as this was what we felt was most needed. We organized a film club, community hangouts, parties (featuring drag performances from the community), one zine and one bisexual conference. In addition, Lilach and I facilitated two bisexual consciousness-raising groups, and I created and administered both a mailing list and a Facebook group for the community (this was in the early days of Facebook, when most activist communication was still done over email).

We made all group decisions through consensus. All our events were either free or pay-what-you-can, and radically inclusive. We were feminists. Most of us were trans and genderqueer, many were people of colour, fat, and disabled. One of the main cores of our politics was solidarity with the Palestine liberation movement, and opposition to Zionism. We supported the Boycott, Divestment, Sanctions (BDS) movement against

Israel Apartheid and were outspoken against pinkwashing – the Israeli government's cynical use of our few hard-won LGBTQ rights in order to paint Israel as a "gay haven" in the Middle East, both drawing attention away from – and justifying – apartheid, military violence and ethnic cleansing. All our events were vegan, in solidarity with the animals imprisoned, tortured and killed as part of the industry treating them as objects for human use, rather than as living beings worthy of life and freedom. One fun part was our rule that every group meeting had to include vegan cake.

Perhaps the peak of our activism was the conference we organized in 2012.[3] This was a two-day event with two tracks of lectures, panels, and workshops in a variety of topics – from local bisexual history, through bisexuality, transness and sex education, to political identities and radical politics. Various fact sheets were hung on the walls about bisexual oppression, male and cishet privileges, the Israel Defense Forces (IDF), animal rights, and more. The event itself was held in a central location, easily accessible by public transport, and the venue was physically accessible. We also made sure to have a safety team to prevent sexual (or other) harassment, as well as safe space guidelines. Not only was participation completely free, but both days included free vegan meals (with gluten-free options).

Panorama fell apart in 2013, after DanVeg, our friend and a central member of the group, tried to kill herself. That year, many of us from Panorama were involved with the Tel Aviv SlutWalk (its second year in Tel Aviv), and made sure to make it both radical and intersectional. After the event, we experienced an unprecedented backlash, with cishet white feminists

---

3   A second conference was held in 2015, organized by a group of activists from Mashriptzot (Sprinklers), the queer anarchist group that many of Panorama's members formed after it stopped its activity.

attacking us for being inclusive of trans and queer women, and of women of colour. The backlash quickly came to focus on DanVeg, for being part of the organizing team while also being assigned male at birth and a person of colour. It lasted for two unrelenting months. It was cruel, and invasive, and after DanVeg's suicide attempt, it burned us out completely. In the end, Panorama stopped its activity because of transmisogyny, queerphobia and racism.

The London Bi Pandas

The London Bi Pandas started out as a spontaneous response to the fact that there was to be no bisexual float in the 2019 London Pride. Though the group existed for less than two years, it managed to make a significant mark and create both discourse and activism that formed a rare distillation of anarchist bi politics.

The float project started a few months before London Pride, when founder Fox al-Rajim heard that there wasn't going to be a bi float that year (the previous year, 2018, was the first time a bi float had ever been included) (Shearing, 2018). With no prior activist experience, they fundraised and gathered people to participate and organize, making the float a grassroots community effort. The float itself was starkly different from ones normally featured in Pride, as the Pandas emphasized not only bi identity, but also radical and intersectional politics. As a subversion of the capitalist and imperialist rainbow-washing of Pride, participants wore mostly black and white (inspired by actual pandas). They held up signs not only protesting biphobia, but also bearing messages like "Guillotine the bankers", "ACAB (All Cops Are Bastards)", "No pride in War", and "No TERFs on our turf" – all centering the message that "Pride is a Protest!"

Though they did face a backlash, the response was largely positive, and gave the Pandas momentum to continue their

activity. Some of their actions included a banner drop protesting the participation of weapons dealer BAE Systems in London Pride and its sponsorship of Surrey Pride, multiple protests
against transphobia and TERFs, and vigils supporting bisexual
asylum seekers. They created an open letter on anti-racism,
which ended up being signed by over a hundred UK LGBTQ
organizations. Once Covid-19 hit, they succeeded in raising over
£20,000 to create a hardship fund, offering direct financial relief to any marginalized LGBTQIA+ person who applied (Moore,
2020). During the lockdowns, they worked on making their website a community activist resource, including guides on dismantling racism, and an ongoing project on resisting transphobia
called "50 Ways to Leave Your TERFer".

In addition to dismantling biphobia and bi erasure, their
stated values included supporting and prioritizing bi+ folks of
marginalized intersectionalities, anti-fascism, anti-capitalism,
Black Lives Matter, supporting bi+ trans+, non-binary and intersex people, and the decriminalization of sex work.

The Pandas' activity was not only limited to outward actions,
but also included community building. They endeavoured to
create a welcoming community space for anyone who wanted
to participate, and so also organized parties, community hang-
outs, Dungeons and Dragons games, a craft club, and more.

The end of London Bi Pandas bears some resemblance to
that of Panorama. According to Fox, over the group's period of
activity, more and more white people had started taking up
space, in a way that was unsustainable and alienated the people of colour who were ultimately the group's core. This came
in addition to an increasing demand of Fox themself to cater to
white needs and feelings within the group, while working in a
full-time job and putting 20–40 additional hours per week into
organizing.

This all came to a head after white activists from the group organized an anti-TERF protest at Grenfell Tower, and set off smoke bombs – without regard for the trauma suffered by the residents (overwhelmingly people of colour) in the 2017 fire. Unsurprisingly, this caused considerable backlash, including coverage by the *Daily Mail* (Howes, 2020). The official Bi Pandas Twitter (now known as X) account posted an apology the day after, and a consultation process was started between members of colour, at the end of which it was decided to dismantle the group.

The Bi Pandas' farewell notice read:

> As our space flooded with more white bodies, we became deeper embedded in white supremacy [...] It's no longer enough for white people to create spaces and try to make them "inclusive". That's not inclusion – that's assimilation and colonisation. It's time for us to resign, step down, step aside, and break what we've created (London Bi Pandas).

And so, much like Panorama, the Bi Pandas stopped their activity because of transmisogyny and racism.

What next?

The similarities between Panorama and the Bi Pandas teach us the importance of creating sustainable activism and communities. In both cases, the overwhelming majority of the work was borne by only one person (Fox in the Bi Pandas, and myself in Panorama), which illustrates both the enormous lack in active bi leadership, and the intense burnout that results. They are also both examples of how "external" forms of oppression can break a community from inside, and how we need to always work on internalized oppression within our communities.

But both groups also show us that anarchabisexuality is possible – that it is viable, and that we can use it to radically change reality. Both Panorama and the London Bi Pandas affected their respective communities and discourses, and created a radical bi activist legacy. The connections that both groups made between bi oppression and other types of oppression can serve as a template for an anarchabisexual movement, how it might look and work. They can serve as models, as inspiration, and as a lesson for future bi activism.

Anarchabisexuality means integrating everything we know about oppression, and using all our power to resist it in the broadest way possible. It means we can believe in a reality where we topple everything – monosexism and biphobia, transphobia, homophobia, misogyny, racism, whiteness, ableism and every other form of oppression. It means acknowledging the ways we can dismantle society, and using everything we know and everything we don't, because we know we can win. Anarchabisexuality can be the most important weapon we have. Let's use it.

References

Balagoon, K. (2019). *A Soldier's Story: Revolutionary Writings by a New Afrikan Anarchist*. The Anarchist Library. https://theanarchistlibrary.org/library/kuwasi-balagoon-a-soldier-s-story.

Eisner, S. (2013). *Bi: Notes for a Bisexual Revolution*. Berkeley, CA: Seal Press.

Howes, S. (2020). "Transgender activists are condemned by Grenfell Tower victims as they set off smoke bombs close to the block where 72 people died." Mail Online, 15 March 2020. www.dailymail.co.uk/

news/article-8112857/Transgender-activists-condemned-Grenfell-victims-set-smoke-bombs-close-block.html.

Kornegger, P. (1975). *Anarchism: The Feminist Connection*. The Anarchist Library. https://theanarchistlibrary.org/library/peggy-kornegger-anarchism-the-feminist-connection.

London Bi Pandas. "Good bye." https://web.archive.org/web/2020 1107061420/https://www.londonbipandas.com. Accessed 4 June 2023.

Mary Nardini Gang. (2009). *Criminal Intimacy*. The Anarchist Library. https://theanarchistlibrary.org/library/mary-nardini-gang-criminal-intimacy.

Mary Nardini Gang. (2014). *Toward the Queerest Insurrection*. The Anarchist Library. https://theanarchistlibrary.org/library/mary-nardini-gang-toward-the-queerest-insurrection.

Moore, M. (2020). "London Bi Pandas raise over £20,000 for vulnerable LGBTQ people." Gay Times, 2 May 2020. www.gaytimes.co.uk/life/london-bi-pandas-raise-over-20000-for-vulnerable-lgbtq-people.

Shearing, L. (2018). "Why London Pride's first bi float was so important." The Queerness, 1 August 2018. https://thequeerness.wordpress.com/2018/08/01/why-london-prides-first-bi-float-was-so-important.

Further reading

Bailey, M. (2013). Homolatent Masculinity and Hip Hop Culture. Moya Bailey, 15 December 2013. www.moyabailey.com/2013/12/15/homolatent-masculinity-and-hip-hop-culture/.

Baroque, F. & Eanelli, T. (eds) (2011). *Queer Ultra Violence: Bash Back! Anthology*. San Francisco, CA: Ardent Press.

Bey, M. (2020). *Anarcho-Blackness: Notes toward a Black Anarchism*. Oakland, CA: AK Press.

Bottici, C. (2021). *Anarchafeminism*. London: Bloomsbury Academic.

Branson, S. (2022). *Practical Anarchism: A Guide for Daily Life*. London: Pluto Press.

Chomsky, N. (2013). *On Anarchism*. New York, NY: The New Press.

Daring, C.B., Rogue, J., Shannon, D. & Volcano, A. (eds) (2013). *Queering Anarchism: Addressing and Undressing Power and Desire*. Oakland, CA: AK Press.

Dark Star Collective. (2012). *Quiet Rumours: An Anarcha-Feminist Reader*. Oakland, CA: AK Press.

Eisner, S. (2012). Love, rage and the occupation: Bisexual politics in Israel/Palestine. *Journal of Bisexuality*, 12(1), 80–137.

Friedland, L. & Highleyman, L.A. (1991). "The Fine Art of Labeling: The Convergence of Anarchism, Feminism, and Bisexuality." In L. Hutchins & L. Ka'ahumanu (eds), *Bi Any Other Name: Bisexual People Speak Out* (pp.285–298). New York, NY: Alyson Publications.

Goldman, E. (1996). *Red Emma Speaks: An Emma Goldman Reader*. Atlantic Highlands, NY: Humanities Press.

Gordon, U. (2008). *Anarchy Alive!: Anti-Authoritarian Politics From Practice to Theory*. London: Pluto Press.

Hunter, A. (2019). "Naked interview with a London Bi Panda." Unicorn Hunting Blog, 20 October 2019. https://web.archive.org/web/20201028053631/https://unicornhunting.blog/naked-interview-london-bi-panda.

"Introducing: Bi Pandas." Freedom, 8 February 2020. https://freedomnews.org.uk/2020/02/08/introducing-bi-pandas.

Mary Nardini Gang. (2009). *What Is It to Become Beautiful?* The Anarchist Library. https://theanarchistlibrary.org/library/mary-nardini-gang-what-is-it-to-become-beautiful.

Mary Nardini Gang. (2014). *Toward the Queerest Insurrection*. The Anarchist Library. https://theanarchistlibrary.org/library/mary-nardini-gang-toward-the-queerest-insurrection.

Mary Nardini Gang. (2019). *Be Gay Do Crime: An Introduction*. The Anarchist Library. https://theanarchistlibrary.org/library/mary-nardini-gang-be-gay-do-crime.

Milstein, C. (2010). *Anarchism and Its Aspirations*. Oakland, CA: AK Press.

Neal, D., Boraas, E., Elkin, G. & McKay, I. (2020). *An Anarchist FAQ: Version 15.4*. The Anarchist Library. https://theanarchistlibrary.org/library/the-anarchist-faq-editorial-collective-an-anarchist-faq-full.

Purkis, J. & Bowen, J. (eds) (1997). *Twenty-First Century Anarchism: Unorthodox Ideas for a New Millennium*. London: Continuum.

Purkis, J. & Bowen, J. (eds) (2012). *Changing Anarchism: Anarchist Theory and Practice in a Global Age*. Manchester: Manchester University Press.

The AmBIssadors. (2020). "The AmBIssadors: Bi+ activism. Part 1." YouTube, 15 September 2020. https://youtu.be/mUHyG7Lyies.

The AmBIssadors. (2020). "The AmBIssadors: What is bi activism? Part 2." YouTube, 12 October 2020. https://youtu.be/DNv_8qioiWU.

"Towards a Rational Bisexuality." *Anarchy*, February 1971, pp.3–8. https://libcom.org/article/anarchy-01-1971.

CHAPTER 14

Religion, Justice and Community

A Bi Pride UK Origin Story
Avi Kay

Avi Kay (they/them) is the co-founder and Chair of Bi Pride UK, a national award-winning charity which creates celebratory and educational spaces for people attracted to more than one gender. Professionally they work in volunteer management in the charity sector, with Bi Pride UK as a side project that got a bit out of hand. Avi is bi/pan, agender, non-binary, demisexual and greyromantic – in queer terms they seem to sit somewhere in the middle of every spectrum! They are also disabled and autistic, and their idea of a good night is a comfy sofa and Netflix. Avi lives in London with their fiancé and two teddy bears, and enjoys singing and cross stitching in their spare time.

Unexpected beginnings

If someone had told me back in February 2017 that the phone call I was about to join would lead to over six years (and counting) of late-night meetings about financial planning, exhausting weekends spent travelling across the UK between full-time work weeks, never-ending circular conversations about why bi people need their own Pride, and long evenings spent writing grant applications, strategies and annual reports, alongside several bipolar episodes, would I still have joined the call?

It might seem like an easy answer – is anything really worth all that? But it's not so simple. Because for every exhausting weekend travelling to Prides, there were dozens of bi people coming away from the Pride feeling validated and welcomed. For every difficult conversation with someone being deliberately antagonistic, I have met so many more wonderful people, some of whom I would now consider among my closest friends. For every long day spent entirely in front of a computer screen, another funder put their trust in us to deliver our ambitious plans.

Being the Chair of Bi Pride UK, currently the largest registered bi charity in the UK, has been a rollercoaster of an experience so far. Where we are now is not where we ever expected or planned to be early on. But the history of how it all came to be starts a while before that February phone call...

The personal is political

I have always been a do-er. I was the kid who always aimed to raise the largest amount of money in my year group for Red Nose Day. I was the teen who joined a peer-led Jewish youth group (RIP AJ6) at 16 and within about a week had been voted on to the executive committee as co-chair of the freshly resurrected Thames Valley region. I was the student who went to a university which didn't have a Jewish Society and so I quickly set about forming one with a friend.

I share this not out of arrogance: it's how I was raised. In her spare time, my mum set up and ran (as a volunteer) a non-profit kosher shop – the only kosher shop in Reading – and volunteered extensively with Macmillan and other charities until shortly before her death. My dad was president of the local synagogue on and off for years, and a school governor.

I'm very aware that it is a middle-class privilege to have the time and resources to do all of this, but for me personally, it's also religious praxis.

The political is religious

I was raised in Orthodox Judaism, and although I left a lot of it behind in my early twenties, there are a few things that I've clung on to, especially *tzedakah*, *tikkun olam* and *tzedek*.

Tzedakah is the practice of giving money to charity. The idea is that you should donate 10 per cent of what you have left after you've accounted for all your needs (in the modern world: rent, bills, food, travel, etc.), up to a maximum of 20 per cent (to avoid risking impoverishing yourself to help others). This has been my favourite Jewish practice ever since I was a young child.

Tikkun olam literally translates as "healing/mending the world", and is a recognition that there is a lot wrong in the world that needs collective effort to be set right. Practically, it means taking action and supporting work which makes things better for others.

Tzedek means justice. If it looks similar to the word *tzedakah*, that's no coincidence: tzedakah is the practice of justice enacted through money. The concept of *tzedek*, for me, points to everything from defunding the police to not crossing picket lines, and is a major driver in why I have only worked in the charity sector so far in my career.

The religious is personal

The sum of these different concepts points in one direction for me: volunteering. When I look at the idea of *tzedakah*, for me it isn't just about giving money; it's also about my time, which is just as valuable a resource to give. To be honest, as someone who works in the charity sector, I have a lot more time to give than I do money! My aim is to volunteer at least 10 per cent of my time after the necessities have been accounted for (work, sleep, eating, etc.), and to do no more than 20 per cent so I have enough time for some self-care too. Though I confess I'm often not great at keeping it as low as 20 per cent...

All of this is to demonstrate that for me, volunteering is an expression of my Jewish practice as well as being something that I generally enjoy doing. But that's not the only way my Judaism underpins the history of my involvement in bi activism – it was also through Judaism that I found my route into queer activism to begin with.

Finding my Jewish voice

The year 2014 was a strange year for me. I was a freshly out as bi, having come out in a very low-key way during my final-year university exams the previous year, but it was also the year I was coming to terms with some religious questions. Just the little ones, you know, like "Is there a God?" and "Do I still want to do the religion that's been at the core of my identity for my entire life?" Ultimately, I found myself making what was literally an overnight decision to leave behind religious practice, or at least to re-evaluate which bits still had a significance in my life as it was reshaping itself.

My experience of Orthodox Judaism had a very strong focus on practice. To a certain extent, it didn't feel as though it mattered too much if I believed in God as long as I followed the practices. What that meant practically, though, is that every part of my life, from what I ate to what I wore to how I allocated my annual leave, was lived Jewishly in some way. As a result, this disentangling process was no small feat.

The Judaism I was raised in was also at its heart dependent on being part of a bigger community, and leaving that behind was an even bigger challenge. There were a lot of people who, overnight, were no longer part of my life. Others didn't actively reject me but I was too worried about being judged by them to stay connected. It was a very isolating experience, and there are still people I miss from those before-times, nine years later.

Finding my queer voice

So as a result of all of this, I found myself subconsciously needing a new community, and consciously needing new outlets for my volunteering. The natural fit was the small world of queer Judaism.

My first Pride was later that year at Pride in London, and I marched with the queer Jews, introduced by my queer Jewish best friend. I was still practising parts of *Shabbat* (the Sabbath from Friday evening into Saturday) at the time, which for me meant not carrying anything with me (especially money) or using public transport, so I walked all the way from where I lived in West Hampstead to the parade muster point on Baker Street. Then after going clubbing that night with old and new friends (who bankrolled me because I didn't even have a bank card on me!), I walked all the way home because, even though *Shabbat* was over, I didn't have any means of paying for the bus or tube back!

From that day, I found a new community, and that's when I started volunteering with KeshetUK, a queer Jewish education charity. I started by training as a facilitator for LGBTQIA+ inclusion trainings run in any Jewish spaces that would have me, and then I joined the volunteer management team as well. As one of few bi volunteers in those days, I found myself contributing to the evolution of how bi identities were covered in training content and included in the organization. And so my bi activism wings were beginning to grow!

It felt especially powerful to be able to contribute in a very small way to a guide on LGBTQIA+ inclusion in Orthodox Jewish schools which was later endorsed by the Chief Rabbi. It was fantastic knowing that the next generations would be learning positive things while coming to terms with their identities at such a formative time in their development. I was and remain so grateful for KeshetUK being there for me at such a formative time in my own development.

Finding my choir voice

The second half of 2015 saw me going through a very bad patch of mental health, and I was diagnosed a few years later as bipolar. Self-care requires a much bigger slice of time when your mental health is at a low ebb, and even 10 per cent of my time volunteering became more than I could manage. As a result, all my volunteering ground to a bit of a halt.

When I turned a corner at the beginning of 2016, I decided it was time I had a non-volunteering hobby in my life, so I started looking into choirs. I was classically trained as a teenager, and singing makes me happy. I remembered watching a choir called the Pink Singers performing on the main stage at Pride in London back at my first Pride and thinking, "I could do that one day." Well, it so happened that they were holding auditions. I had a go, and got in!

Joining the Pinkies was a bit overwhelming to begin with. I've never been good at big groups, and the choir was 90 strong! I was also one of very few bi members at the time (that I knew of), so I relied on something I was used to: going hard on bi inclusion in a majority gay space. I overheard (or received directly) a fair few biphobic comments, and as someone who's never shied away from conflict, I spoke up every time. There can be a big difference between what an organization's policies say and what some of its individual members think, and I tried to contribute on both sides of that equation. It was a bit of a microcosm of wider LGBTQIA+ spaces – in some ways it was quite isolating to feel othered and out of place, but I also saw the power of community through it as other bi members started coming out to me as they saw someone being vocal and visible.

One thing that turned out to be life-changing was knowingly meeting my first bi person over the age of 30. As an over-30s bi who's been in bi spaces for a while now, it's easy to forget that for 24-year-old me, this was seismic. But up until that point, although I knew full well that being bi wasn't a phase, I had only encountered younger bis. In that reality, it's hard not to internalize the classic biphobic myths about bi people

– ultimately, "choosing a gender". But no, here was an older bi, happily settled in a long-term relationship, still vocally declaring their bi identity. It was something that Younger Me didn't realize until then that they really needed to see.

The other way in which this friendship was life-changing was that she told me about her friend Hannah-Rose Tristram, who had had an idea for a one-off Bi Pride event, and made the virtual introduction between us. I loved the idea, and given my history of trying to get things done, I was keen to get it off the ground, but first I needed to take my first steps into the bi community itself.

Finding my bi activist voice

In July 2016, I attended the first Stonewall Bi Role Models Day. Everyone in the room, including facilitators, identified in some way as attracted to more than one gender, and it was the first time I had knowingly been in a room with more than a handful of bi people. I'd never been in a totally bi space. There was something immediately liberating about the shared experiences which didn't need to be explicitly named, while also having rich diversity in the space. Across the day, we explored what it means to have and to be a role model, and I came away feeling empowered and keen to channel my energies into something.

I started small, with some more internal bi inclusion work with KeshetUK, and going to more bi community events and spaces. In the meantime, Hannah-Rose and I kept chatting and bouncing ideas around. It was clear pretty quickly that we were going to need more than just the two of us to get things off the ground, so we set up a call to get as many people who might be interested in the idea of a Bi Pride together as possible. And that's how I came to be joining that call in 2017 which would open a new chapter in my life.

Turning ideas into ambitions

We covered a lot of ground in the first few calls, trying to determine what appetite there was for a Pride event specifically for our community. There were so many things to consider: where the event would take place, how it would be funded, when it should be... Unsurprisingly, there were a lot of opinions about everything!

Having seeded the idea, Hannah-Rose stepped back, and I stepped first into a co-chair role alongside a passionate team of other volunteers. We had a long journey ahead of us, and soon the ideas and the ambitions started to grow. First was the hope that there would be enough interest to make it an annual repeating event. Then plenty of people raised the point that the Pride movement across the UK was growing massively, and bi inclusion needed to be at the heart of this growth for us to be serving our community as it deserves. A new education and outreach area of work evolved, looking beyond our event to increase bi inclusion throughout the year and across the UK. And even with this, we also quickly acknowledged that there would always be people who, for many reasons, might be excluded from participation in physical spaces, so a communications team focused on building online and virtual spaces was also essential.

We therefore soon had three pillars of work to focus on, all needing to work separately and together to build educational and celebratory spaces for the bi communities. By this point, we had far outgrown the earliest ideas, and it was clear that we needed a lot more infrastructure than a committee of enthusiastic activists, and ways to access funding that would be almost impossible without a formal structure. We looked to the charity sector.

Turning ambitions into a charity

As a teenager, I always aspired one day to set up a charity, but Teenage Me would definitely have been surprised to find that it was going to be a queer charity, given that they hadn't quite twigged on to the queer thing just yet!

What was to become Bi Pride UK wasn't my first dabble in charity governance. Along with seeking a new hobby at the beginning of 2016, I also undertook my first trustee position. I wanted to gain a new perspective in my charity sector career, especially learning about charity governance, strategic planning and fiscal management. Five months and ten days later, I was one of the last trustees standing at Broken Rainbow UK when it went into voluntary liquidation. As hobbies go, it turned out to be a pretty stressful one! In my short tenure, the main lesson I learned was how not to run a charity. A valuable lesson, but hard-earned.

So, when we decided to go for charity status, with me as the sole chair by that point, I had a fair amount of trepidation. Somehow, though, the process of registering as a charity was one of the easiest parts of our journey. The day in February 2018 that we learned we were officially a registered charity was the best day of my life to date, only to be overtaken by our first Bi Pride itself – but I'm getting ahead of myself.

The challenges of geography

A big question we grappled with was where to run our Bi Pride. As a one-off event, it made most sense to put it somewhere with a large and active queer population. But as a repeat event, we had the choice of keeping it in the same place each year or moving it around the country to reach new and more geographically diverse audiences. Ultimately, we put Bi Pride in London for the short to medium term, but we're still open to the possibility of future events being elsewhere.

Because of that decision, though, we feel a responsibility to invest in bi communities outside the capital. In both 2018 and 2019, we attended about 30 Prides across the UK. Where there was a local bi group, we joined with their plans and provided financial support where possible, and where there was no local bi organization we marched or ran a stall ourselves to raise bi visibility. It is out on the road at local Prides that moves me most – getting to interact with all the people who are just so excited to be seen, acknowledged and celebrated is a powerful reminder of the importance of visibility. I'm delighted that we were able to start returning to this model in 2023.

We also planned to pilot Bi Pride Local in May 2020, bringing some of what the flagship Bi Pride event offers to places outside London. The first event was to be a collaboration with Bi Cymru, working with them to enlarge the well-established BiFest Wales event. Our funding and infrastructure would have enabled Bi Cymru to pay event speakers and contributors a fee for their time and make attendance free for everyone. Unfortunately, these plans were disrupted by the pandemic, but we hope to re-launch Bi Pride Local in the not-too-distant future!

The challenges of ethical fundraising

The corporatization of Pride was a big elephant in the room. We didn't want to be yet another space for companies to put their logo on and in the process lose sight of the most important stakeholder: our bi communities. However, we also knew from the outset that being a free-to-attend event was a non-negotiable accessibility principle, and putting on a Pride doesn't come cheap, especially in London. In the early days, as a green team of enthusiastic volunteers, we wanted to be a Pride which didn't take any corporate money, but it became apparent pretty quickly that this was going to make the project very difficult. I also recall a pivotal conversation I had with a bi activist in which they pointed out that corporates have money earmarked for queer causes and it's better that they underwrite work for our communities than bi individuals having to stump up that money from their own limited funds. That point totally shifted my perspective on the issue and I remember it often.

Historically, the bi community sees very little of the money that goes to queer organizations. With businesses and grant-makers often having a hefty due diligence process for funding, and very few bi organizations having some kind of formal structure like charity status, informal groups of activists are often left behind. That's before you even factor in the huge amount of time it takes to build corporate relationships and to apply for grant funding, time that small teams of activists often just don't have to spare. However, we had a package of event sponsorship that we knew would be appealing to businesses, and a charity registration number to provide the high-level credibility needed. It was worth taking advantage of those things for the sake of the community, and for that rare thing in activism: a sustainable income source.

Choosing to take corporate money was not the same as accepting money indiscriminately, though. We developed an ethical fundraising policy laying out which industries we would never take money from, including arms manufacturers, the oil industry, and a few others. The policy also requires every potential corporate partner to pass through an in-depth due diligence process, involving a deep dive into the company's connections and internal circumstances and a request for information not in the public domain. This process is important from a reputational perspective, but it is also an ethical stance and is a lot more than a rubber stamp. We only work with companies where the impact for their bi staff and an internal commitment to improving experiences for more marginalized identities within their staff team is evident. Even in our earliest days when we were scrabbling for pennies, we preferred to look elsewhere for income than to take it from some of the businesses who reached out to us.

The challenges of proving a concept

Aside from logistical and ethical challenges, some (both within and beyond the bi communities) felt that a Bi Pride event was a separatist venture. The concern was that it would make other Prides less likely to bother putting work into bi inclusion because bi people could just go to their own Pride. Some also feared that it would give the impression that bi people want to be separate from the wider queer community rather than an integral part of it.

Others were concerned that there wouldn't be sufficient demand for a whole Bi Pride event. Although most Prides start off fairly small, they are still perceived as, and are usually intended to be, mass participation events, and bi community organizing in the UK had typically been focused on smaller-scale events until that point. Even by putting Bi Pride in London, with a large population to draw from, people questioned whether it would be able to attract more than a few hundred people.

And then there were questions about whether a Pride-shaped event would even fit what the well-established bi communities wanted. The concept of a "Pride event" conjures up some strong images and, especially for bi people, some of these images can carry trauma. Bi people are very used to hearing people, and even performers, making biphobic "jokes" and digs at mainstream Pride events. This is coupled with the fact that a lot of Prides are also heavily corporate in nature, with the queer community feeling muscled out of its own spaces by rainbow capitalism. If these are the impressions you have of Pride and you transfer that image into a Pride specifically for bi communities, it's understandable that there would be some resistance.

Some of these concerns we addressed head on, showing what we were doing to put community at the heart of our event and to work towards bi inclusion in other Prides, and some we recognized we would only be able to dispel by giving it a go and seeing what happened. Ultimately, bi people would vote with their feet. If it fell flat, well, that would be that. But if it succeeded, we would have brought something new and good to our communities.

From a personal perspective, I also faced the challenge of proving my credentials within the community. Although I had been involved in queer activism for many years, I was a relative newcomer to bi activism. There I was leading a newly registered charity populated by other bi activism newbies which was bringing an entirely untested concept to the community space, but I had a professional background in charities and a determination to see where a concept could go when it had charity status behind it. At times, it felt like an uphill battle. It would be impossible to share all the challenges we and I have experienced over the years – but it has been worth the persistence!

Making history with Pride

Throughout everything, we have tried to have the bi communities' interests and hopes at the heart of our work, and the principles of accessibility and representation as our driving force.

And so we arrived at last at our 2019 Pride, which was a fantastic event, the culmination of the hard work of hundreds of volunteers across two-and-a-half years. The focal parts of Bi Pride included a Main Stage, with musicians, comedians and other performers, the I Am Proud Stage, with panels on a range of topics such as the experiences of racialized bi people, being bi in the workplace and how bi identities are represented on screen, and a Community Hub, with stalls run by bi community activists, queer charities and our corporate sponsors.

With over 1300 people attending, it was the biggest single-day bi event that the world had ever seen, and feedback from attendees and contributors was overwhelmingly positive. For me, it was without question the best day of my life. I'm so proud of what we managed to achieve at the event, but also glad of what we learned from it that we could do better.

Taking Pride in accessibility

We invested significant resources in the event's access features.

A grant from the LGBT+ Futures Fund paid for British Sign Language (BSL) interpreters for both the Main Stage's performers and the I Am Proud stage's panels, roaming BSL interpreters for anyone who needed them, and a Mobiloo providing a toilet with a changing bench, hoist and attendant for those who need more assistance than a regular accessible toilet can provide. There were ear defenders available for attendees to borrow free of charge, and we set aside a room as a quiet sensory space, with equipment borrowed from Coventry Pride. We provided a changing room for trans people and anyone who wasn't able to travel to the event in the clothes they felt comfortable expressing themselves through; we made all toilets gender neutral, and had free sanitary products available for anyone who needed them. We had free water stations throughout the site, and entry to the event itself was free.

There were also things we didn't get right. In particular, we had a beautiful venue in the Round Chapel in Hackney, but as an old building, its physical accessibility was more of an add-on than built into the fabric of the building. This meant that our step-free access route through the venue became harder to navigate at busier times during the event, and we should have allocated more volunteers to ensure that this was constantly monitored. We also found that the routes between and around areas of the site became quite congested at busier times, again making navigating the event challenging. Having a busier event than expected was certainly not a bad thing, but we learned that we needed to be prepared for this and to ensure that our next venue (having outgrown the Round Chapel after just one event!) would have space for everything without getting congested, with step-free access available at all times and dedicated access volunteers on hand to help anyone who needed assistance to navigate the site.

The other access challenge that we grappled with was how to reconcile a one-day event in London with the reality of a bi community spread out across the UK. We knew there would be so many reasons why people were unable to attend, whether they couldn't take time off work or from caring responsibilities, were unable to travel because of a disability, weren't yet out to those around them – the list goes on. However, the process of adapting to Covid restrictions and running online events in 2020 and 2021 showed us a solution to some of these challenges.

Bringing Pride back

I cannot adequately describe how it felt to be able to return to a physical Bi Pride event at last. As we are a charity which runs a mass participation event, Covid was a major obstacle, especially since we were only able to run one Pride event before the world changed. Our virtual events (the BiFi Festival in June 2020, Let's Get Visible in September 2020, and a virtual Bi Pride in September 2021) were amazing outpourings of community, exploring topics of the day, but there is something incredible about having hundreds of bi people together in one place that a purely online event can't replicate.

Our Bi Pride event in September 2022 on the Mile End campus of Queen Mary's, University of London, took the same format as our 2019 event, with two stages and a Community Hub. However, it had one significant addition: both stages were live streamed on our social media channels. This meant that people who were unable to come to the event for any reason, including Covid caution, could watch what was going on from anywhere in the world. People could also catch up on most of the content later if they weren't available while it was being streamed live, as it was recorded at the same time. By investing in this, we were able to bring Bi Pride to a much wider audience. Between in-person attendees and those joining us online, we had 1300 with us again on the day, and we only see this number growing in years to come.

No event is ever perfect. We identified things we can improve on for future events (assuming that we don't find ourselves in another lockdown!), and we are confident that each year will build on the ones before, offering the Pride space that our bi communities deserve.

Looking back, looking forwards

Our first six or so years have seen a lot more than we could ever have expected, and we're excited to look to the future. We have tried throughout to be driven by our community and to ensure that as we grow, we put that growth back into the bi activists and organizations around us.

We're very excited about having launched a Bi Community Fund in partnership with Consortium, which provides micro grants with a low-effort application process for bi activism across the UK. While it's in pilot form now, with most of the funds in the pot provided by us, we hope to see future rounds of the programme with bigger funders. The impact of these micro grants will be vast – a small amount of money like £100 might be virtually meaningless to a large queer charity, but for bi activists it could make all the difference. We have a lot of power and privilege as a registered charity with access to funding, and it's our duty to make sure we are using that power for the benefit of unfunded bi activists and organizations. The Bi Community Fund is one of our ways of doing that.

We have lots of ambitions for the years to come. We hope that our flagship Bi Pride event will grow, but more importantly that it will become more accessible every year, and one day maybe we'll have a Bi Pride march as well as the venue-based event. We want to deepen our engagement with local bi groups, hopefully with a relaunched Bi Pride Local bringing more educational and celebratory spaces outside London. And one day, who knows, it might not be too big a dream to have a paid staff team running the charity too, creating paid bi activism jobs!

On a personal level, I'm excited to think about the future. I have poured heart and soul into Bi Pride UK for all these years – I've described it as my baby or my spouse at different times. But for me, the most important thing is to get the charity to a point where I can hand on the chair role to someone else who will bring new and fresh ideas. So many charities can end up being a cult of personality if the founder sticks around too long, and I want to avoid that. Our achievements are just that: ours, not mine. And I look forward to the day when I can just be an attendee (well, okay, more likely an on-the-day volunteer!) at Bi Pride, with the organization and the event in the capable hands of the next generation.

So, all in all, would I go back in time to warn my past self not to join that fateful call in February 2017? Absolutely not! I think my message would be "This is going to change your life, so give it your best, ignore the doubts and detractors, and have fun!"

CHAPTER 15

The Living Room

On Building An Alternate Bisexual Reality

Bren Frederick

Bren Frederick (any pronouns) is a genderqueer bisexual activist, podcast producer and graphic designer. In 2020, she founded the Bi Pan Library, a grassroots queer archive preserving the literary history of the bi, pan and m-spec community. She makes her home in Washington State, USA with her partner, their three cats, and several thousand books. You can find her on IG at @brenfrederick.

We're here now

Have you ever been in a place where history becomes tangible? Where you stand motionless, feeling time and importance press around you, press into you? (Becky Chambers, *To Be Taught, If Fortunate*, 2019, p.19)

I have created an alternate reality in my living room. At first glance, it's nothing exceptional. There's a well-worn black loveseat, a hand-braided rug I made out of scrap fabric, and a side table loaded with paperbacks. Lining one wall are five floor-to-ceiling bookshelves ($35 each on sale, I always tell visitors), heavy with more books. On the opposite wall is a large wooden desk, papers, pencils and envelopes and stacks of more books littered across it, accented with a beautiful robin's-egg velvet chair that took me months of penny-pinching to buy. Every corner of the room is cozy, solid...and mundane. To find the magic, the something-special, the space-and-time-defying power, that requires you to take a closer look.

You see, if you are bi or pan or otherwise attracted to people of multiple genders, the 1000+ books here can transport you to a world in which you do not have to fight to be acknowledged. Go to the bookshelves and pick a book – any book! Sit down to read it, and find someone like you. A biromantic college student,[1] or a pansexual detective,[2] or a real-life children's book author who fervently loved men and women throughout her lifetime.[3] Pick a book from my favourite shelf, far away from the window so the sunshine does not touch it, and find the words of bi and pan activists from as far back as the 1960s, transcribed oral histories, and bi newsletters from the 1970s–1990s, carefully stored in clear sleeves. Snoop around in my secretary desk and find a tin containing hundreds of pinback buttons, a box full of m-spec[4] zines, and home-printed tri-fold brochures recommending non-fiction titles. Look around the room, recognize

---

1   Claire Kann, *Let's Talk about Love*, 2019.

2   Alexis Hall, *The Affair of the Mysterious Letter*, 2019.

3   Amy Gary, *The Great Green Room: The Brilliant and Bold Life of Margaret Wise Brown*, 2017.

4   "M-spec" is short for "multiple-attraction spectrum" or "multisexual spectrum", an inclusive umbrella term for the many different ways people express attraction beyond gender. M-spec includes people who use words for themselves such as bi, pan, omni, fluid, flexible, curious, and more, as well as some people who don't use labels at all.

the wealth at your fingertips, take a breath...and you've arrived in the alternate reality that is the Bi Pan Library.

For eight years I have panned for gold in dusty bookshops and online databases to create this experimental space where my friends and I didn't feel like an afterthought, a hyper-local version of what academic Clare Hemmings has called "concrete bisexual ground" (2002, p.14). If you have a moment to sit with me, I'd love to share with you how this room came to be, how living in this space has altered my own perspectives, and how I hope the physical consolidation of our history can empower the m-spec community as we build new futures.

We exist

> When there's people around that we don't trust, we let them think we're the kinds of people who are allowed to exist. (Sarah Gailey, *Upright Women Wanted*, 2020, p.28)

The first time I read a bisexual book, I was in church. My boy-friend worked in the sound booth for a local non-denominational congregation, the kind that owns a fog machine. I used to tag along with him for worship service rehearsals and wander the empty building until I found a quiet place to nest with a book. The funny thing about growing up a good Christian volunteer is that the building continues to feel like a second home even after you have begun to lose faith, which I had. It was peace-ful when nobody else was around. I knew what my place was here – or I did until this new book entered my life. In *Far from You* by Tess Sharpe (2014), our teenage main character Sophie is mourning and investigating the death of her best friend and secret girlfriend, Mina. When I turned a page and read "she kisses me...", my life flashed in front of my eyes. The best friend I had in elementary school, her big brown eyes and strong arms. The girl from my homeschool co-op who chopped her hair off and painted butterflies on her face. The nights I had spent sobbing and pressing myself into the corner of my room thinking nobody would ever, ever love me if they knew what I knew. The church was closed and the halls were empty, but I felt pinned by a blazing spotlight, lit up for the whole congregation to see. But then, it wasn't just a girlfriend...as I kept reading, Sophie develops a new romantic relationship with a boy. I remembered how many times I had counted every boy I ever thought was cute in hopes of absolving myself. I'm not gay! I liked him, and him, and him...! At the time, I had no word for liking someone no matter which side of the gender-segregated youth group they sat on. I had thought I could stay safe with a nonsense maths equation – if number of boys > number of girls, gay ≠ me. But *Far from You* introduced a devastating new variable. Bisexual. A concept like the holy trinity, one person existing as multiple things at once. My absolution evaporated and I finished the whole book in one sitting, power-reading as if my eyes could outpace the omniscience of God.

At first I didn't confide in anybody other than the algorithms. I followed bisexual YouTubers and took Kinsey scale quizzes. On Google Docs, I kept an untitled running list of books I heard were bisexual, a word I whispered even in the privacy of my own mind. I even made queer friends online, kind people who let me sit on the fringes of their community without coming out or stating my business. One of those queer friends, Rowan, was from England, a lesbian activist and educator who I thought was the smartest person I'd ever met (I still think this). She visited me in the US one summer and we took endless buses back and forth, adventuring across the city. That week it was immensely difficult to remember I was supposed to be straight. Rowan felt like family, and for the first time I wanted someone to know who I really was. The pressure to tell her built up to almost-bursting until the day we visited a local queer library. I tried to look casual while rifling through the section labelled BISEXUAL in white tape. There were just seven books in the section. *Bisexuality: A Critical Reader* (Storr, 1999), *Bisexuality and the Challenge to Lesbian Politics* (Rust, 1995)...they were old and dusty and felt controversial in the diffused glow of a rainbow flag in the window.

That growing enthusiasm to come out to my friend retreated, and I wondered if maybe there wasn't as much space in the LGBTQ+ community for me as I hoped there was. It was wrong to be bisexual in the community that raised me...was it wrong here too? Or were there just not that many people like me? After Rowan flew home to England and I was able to reflect on the trip, I regretted not taking a photo of that shelf. Maybe if I read those books, I could answer all my own questions. In the process of reconstructing the list of titles with the sheer force of Google, I stumbled across *How Queer! Personal Narratives from Bisexual, Pansexual, Polysexual, Sexually-Fluid, and Other Non-Monosexual Perspectives* (Beauchemin, 2016), an anthology collecting 14 short essays by m-spec people, including a few people with conservative Christian backgrounds similar to my own. *How Queer!* became my first true exploration of fluid attraction outside fiction, and it led me to older bisexual essay collections; I devoured *Getting Bi: Voices of Bisexuals around the World* (Ochs & Rowley, 2005), *Rec.og.nize: The Voices of Bisexual Men* (Ochs & Williams, 2014), and *Bi Lives: Bisexual Women Tell Their Stories* (Orndorff, 1999), desperate to hear from the new family I suddenly had all across the globe.

We've got work ahead of us

Out of the sad sack of sad shit that was my life, I made a word-house. (Lidia Yuknavitch, *The Chronology of Water*, 2011, p.201)

Fast forward a year later and my personal landscape was transformed beyond recognition. I had moved out of my parents' house, gotten married, given myself an undercut, and come out as bisexual to everyone I trusted. I felt loved and accepted in ways I had never experienced before. But still, there was something missing. As I separated myself from the deeply conservative world of my upbringing, I couldn't seem to find purchase in a new queer-centric space.

While discovering my bisexuality I had also discovered my rapidly progressing chronic illness, and soon began using a cane and a wheelchair whenever I left the house. Although there was a small and social bi community in my area, I couldn't safely attend their bar meet-ups or movie nights or burlesque shows. Attending my first Pride festival was a disaster. Only half the outdoor venue was wheelchair accessible, and an able-bodied friend had to advocate for me in the dense crowds by shouting "WHEELCHAIR! Coming through!" It was humiliating – not because I was ashamed of my mobility aid, but because of how clear it was that disabled queer people weren't considered valuable enough to proactively include. There seemed to be no way to enter queer spaces without announcing my disabilities to the room and making myself inconvenient to everyone involved. As Leah Lakshmi Piepzna-Samarasinha puts it in *Care Work: Dreaming Disability Justice*, "in so many hip queer communities that are not explicitly disabled, it's not okay to not be okay" (2018, p.199). And so, turned away from in-person community, I invented a new way of nurturing my newly discovered identity: data entry.

My unwieldy Google doc of bisexual books turned into a spreadsheet, tracking data such as publication years, target age groups, and publishing houses. I kept detailed notes of how each book fit my then-nebulous inclusion criteria. The breadth of my interest expanded – I noted pansexual characters, books that never mentioned a label but clearly portrayed multiple-gender attraction, and historical figures whose life paths hinted at fluidity. Before long, the collection jumped off the page and onto my bookshelves. I took my spreadsheet to the thrift store and scoured their shelves for cheap copies, striking true gold one day when I found *Bisexual Politics: Theories, Queries, and Visions* (Tucker, 1996) wedged under the memoir shelf as if someone had tried to hide it. I became a menace at my local used bookstores, where I would make a beeline for their LGBTQ+ section and make a game of flipping to the back of each non-fiction book to see how many times the word "bisexual" was listed in the index.

I also learned I was, delightfully, not the first person to curate an m-spec library digitally or physically! The same year I read my first bisexual book, Kerri Price had begun the Bibliography project inspired by Robyn Ochs' (1995) booklist in the *The Bisexual Resource Guide*, and the Bi Writers Association, helmed by Sheela Lambert, had already been curating a physical bisexual library for a decade. Their work (done in public) encouraged me to see my own work (done in private) in a new light. The collection was my personal property, gathered to support my own sense of identity...but it began to feel symbolic. There were plenty of other disabled pansexuals and small-town biromantics and late-in-life questioners whose first access to queer community might be found on a page. I wanted to help share everything I had found with the world – all the comfort, all the belonging, all the connection to history. Late one night when my partner came home from his second job, we lay in bed and I told him about the vision I had of a room you could walk into and be surrounded by books that acknowledged the existence of multiple attraction. Maybe I could host pop-up installments in queer spaces to invite people to browse the shelves and learn about m-spec history! Or a bookmobile, to travel further! Or perhaps I could collaborate with the queer archive in the city, whose bisexual offerings were limited...would they even be interested? My partner said, "One way or another, you can do something bigger with this." I thought maybe he was right.

In 2020, just as I was gathering courage to invite others into my work, the first Covid-19 case in the US was identified in my county and my health unravelled even further. The pandemic caused worldwide shortages of my life-sustaining medication, and without my prescription I descended into excruciating pain, fever, and dangerously erratic vitals for months. It seemed very possible I could die. When I was lucid, all I could think about was how intensely I regretted never making my research public. I hazily remember lying on my partner's chest one morning and scribbling sloppy lists of document passwords and the email addresses of queer friends who might be willing to keep my work going if the worst happened.

The worst, it should be obvious, did not happen. But I came out the other side a different person; I was physically weaker, deeply traumatized, and the fever in my body had crystallized fear into furious motivation. Everything happened very quickly from there. Friends donated money to secure a proper url, I crafted a handful of webpages, and Bipanlibrary.com made its public debut in October 2020. The website and I were riddled with flaws, but alive.

We're in this together

> I am left with an appreciation of human malleability and the
> ability to push against constraints – social constraints tied
> to...a slew of oppressive beliefs about sexuality and gender.
> When people can successfully navigate these constraints, op-
> pressions, and fears, and come out the other side feeling au-
> thentic and truly themselves, it is worthy of celebration. (Karen
> Morgaine, *Pansexuality: A Panoply of Co-Constructed Narratives,*
> 2019, pp.205–6)

Now that you know how all these books ended up in my living
room, let's talk about what they can do.

My favourite Bi Pan Library service is virtual research consultation, when I sit down over video chat with an author, or a
student, or anyone else who is very very curious, and chat about
their topic of choice. Together we look through the shelves, reference the library's notes, and search through indexes or bibli-
ographies to create a curated reading list that serves their needs.
If a book is out of print, I'll sometimes send limited scans of the
material or transcribe quotes relevant to their subject of interest. This process would normally cost the other person a lot of
time, or travel, or money, or all of the above, but those barriers
are demolished when all the books are in one place and help
is offered freely over a wifi connection. For an hour (or two, or
three), library visitors from all over the planet can absorb the
library's meaning and take a piece of it into their own world.

The magic powering this little alternate reality is that the
books are together, condensed into something potent and in-
vigorating. I estimate at least 90 per cent of the m-spec non-
fiction ever published is on the Bi Pan Library shelves, and when
packed so closely together, these books begin to talk to each

other. Pick up one book and you will find a reference to another book on the shelf below it, then that book will reference an older book from the top shelf, and soon you'll start recognizing names — Lani Ka'ahumanu, H. Sharif Williams, Debra Kolodny, Brett Beemyn, Shiri Eisner, David Lourea, Fritz Klein, June Jordan. The volumes together become larger than the sum of their pages, and a century-long timeline of m-spec heritage begins to take shape.

Read the work of long-time queer activists and you'll often find their views now are very different from when they began in 1970 or 1990 or 2010. They may identify with different words, thanks to our expanded modern vocabulary, or call to erase hard lines they had previously drawn. So whenever you read an older queer text, it helps to bring a curious generosity with you. What work was being built on at the time this book was published? What had already been said, and what was a new idea? Who were the author's peers at the time? If an idea seems harmful, what conversations were the harmed groups having about the idea at the time? What words that we use today didn't exist then, and what words were being used instead? These are all questions the library taught me to ask, and they have helped me and my library visitors not only in the stacks but in the churning oversimplification machine that is social media.

Although my work with the Bi Pan Library is made possible by a wifi connection and I have found invaluable queer friendships online, it is inescapable how cruel the internet can be to m-spec people. We are the butt of jokes from all sides, low-hanging fruit for malicious speculation and harassment. I believe this treatment encourages us towards misinformation and infighting, especially when we are young and first exploring identities. In her 1992 essay "Requiem for the Champ", bisexual poet and teacher June Jordan wrote of growing up poor and Black in Brooklyn, "This is the meaning of poverty: when you have nothing better to do than to hate somebody who, just exactly like yourself, has nothing better to do than to pick on you instead of trying to figure out how come there's nothing better to do" (2002, p.122). As a group, m-spec people are kept poor in terms of personal finance[5] and social aid, on top of the systemic inequality and violence already faced by the high number of disabled[6] and racialized[7] m-spec people. I say *kept poor* because it is true on many levels – in 2017–2018, "projects focused on the specific needs of Bisexual communities again received less than 1% of the total funding" (Global Philanthropy Project, 2020, p.43) provided for LGBTQ+ government and philanthropic programmes.

Choices are made by people with power and, malicious or not, these choices foster an environment of m-spec lack. When we are this starved for resources, it is tempting to allow our pain to morph into resentment towards anybody who seems to be getting the spotlight we feel we're "next in line" for – even if that person is also m-spec, as we see in the repetitive and self-destructive conflicts between bisexual and pansexual communities online. Allying ourselves with our neighbours takes patience, and we're in short supply. Lashing out at whoever is

---

5 "Approximately 25% of bisexual men and 30% of bisexual women live in poverty, compared to 15% and 21% of heterosexual men and women respectively and 20% and 23% of gay man and lesbians" (Movement Advancement Project, 2014, p.2).

6 "The prevalence of disability is higher among lesbian, gay and bisexual adults compared with their heterosexual counterparts; lesbian, gay and bisexual adults with disabilities are significantly younger than heterosexual adults with disabilities" (Fredriksen-Goldsen, Kim & Barkan, 2012, p.e16).

7 "People of colour are more likely to identify as bisexual, compared to their white counterparts" (Movement Advancement Project, 2016, p.i).

standing closest promises immediate gratification, but once the adrenaline fades...what have we gained? And what have we lost?

In many modern efforts to reduce stigma and assure each other of our validity, activists from younger generations, like myself, can unwittingly alienate older generations who lived through remarkably different times and places. It is difficult, for instance, to claim that the Bisexual Manifesto of 1991 proves bisexuality has "never been transphobic" without erasing decades of trans m-spec people's lived experiences. We should combat the idea that bisexuality is entirely "binary", but who do we leave out in the cold by presenting the issue so simply? My dear friend and mentor Corey Alexander once shared with me their painful experience searching for a trans-friendly bisexual community in the 1990s, where they were confronted with such virulent transphobia that they were turned off using the word "bisexual" for themself. In a blog post about this experience, they wrote that they "felt pushed out, like I was being rejected from bisexual community because of my gender and the shape of my desire, a shape that didn't fit the molds created in a ciscentric framework" (West (Alexander), 2016). It took time to absorb this story, but it has become a bedrock of my approach to bisexual history and activism. As queer creative Abigail Thorn has said, "We can think about two things at once." (Philosophy Tube, 2022). Corey's experience does not erase trans people who claim bisexuality for themselves, or the many instances in which transgender and bisexual people allied themselves towards common goals. We simply have different parts of the story to tell.

In her transcendent memoir *In the Dream House*, Carmen Maria Machado (2019) breaks the queer community's public silence on abuse in same-sex relationships, asserting in her chapter about queer villainy:

> We deserve to have our wrongdoing represented as much as our heroism, because when we refuse wrongdoing as a possibility for a group of people, we refuse their humanity. That is to say, queers – real-life ones – do not deserve representation, protection, and rights because they are morally pure or upright as a people. They deserve those things because they are human beings, and that is enough (p. 47).

If we are to move forward into an altered reality, a changed future, we cannot redact everything that makes us uncomfortable about the past. The online panopticon[8] tries to convince us that queer people could lose our claim to resources or rights if we allow our community to be complicated, tempting us to simplify our history so we do not become poorer than we already are. "Fear makes liars of us all," as Machado says (2019, p.44). Our community has certainly earned the fear we carry, but we lose twice when we sacrifice our heritage to escape that fear.

We do not need to demand answers that fit within a 280-character limit or erase stories that do not directly serve our agenda. We can have more than this. June Jordan showed us the way forward in "Requiem for the Champ" (2002, p.121), writing:

> I only learned, last year, that I can stop any violence that starts with me. I only learned, last year, that love is infinitely more interesting, and more exciting, and more powerful, than really winning or really losing a fight. I only learned, last year, that all war leads to death and that all love leads you away from death.

---

8   The panopticon is a form of discipline introduced by philosopher Jeremy Bentham. Prisoners are kept constantly in view of a central observational point, never sure if they are being watched or not, which creates a paranoid self-policing environment.

With effort and humility, we can reject our competitive instincts and lead our conversations with loving curiosity. By freeing ourselves from the endless defensive scramble and confronting our failures as readily as our strengths, we can create new and exciting paths. We can gather the pain and anger – ours and that of others – hold these broken things in our hands, and repair them.

This is why I believe a visual consolidation of our literary history is such a powerful thing, and it is also why I never characterize my work as dealing in "good representation". The Bi Pan Library's shelves intentionally hold ugly stereotypical narratives alongside ground-breaking affirmative works. The alternate reality in my living room is not about relentless positivity, but instead the revolutionary act of m-spec people seeing ourselves as fully human, fully worthy of love, and fully capable of creating a future in which we thrive.

While we're talking about honesty and complication and fear, I want to say that writing this chapter was difficult because I cannot prevent a certain meta flavour from seeping into the narrative. I am uncomfortably aware that whatever I turn in to the publisher will incorporate itself into the library's alternate reality, and in 40 years someone tracing the m-spec movement of the 2020s might read what I've written through the lens of progress we can only dream of today. It is very tempting to fall back into that defensive stance, over-explaining my choices and burying my points in context until I'm saying nothing at all. In her exploratory book of interviews *Pansexuality: A Panoply of Co-Constructed Narratives* (2019), Professor Karen Morgaine describes our struggle to communicate about gender and sexual variance as "trying to hold onto a snake – just when we think we have a grip, it squirms and slips out of our hands (or bites us!)" (p.21). It seems to me the snake, a gloriously flexible and unpredictable creature, is doing exactly what its body was made to do. So instead of desperately trying to control future opinion, I have simply written what I know and believe at this moment, and look forward to whatever beautiful wriggling change comes down the line...even if it comes with fangs.

We're so beautiful

Even if I never read another book, I'm still a person with intrinsic value, and later I'll be a river. (Daniel Lavery, *Something That May Shock and Discredit You*, 2020, p.81)

The Bi Pan Library has given me the gift of open-handed confidence in who I am and where I belong, something I could never have imagined for myself when I sat alone in that church. In-person queer community is still largely inaccessible to me, but I have created my own affirming space that has just as much room for my body when I am well as when I am unwell. I owe thanks to the fiction authors who showed me the path and the personal stories of fellow m-spec people who taught me to walk down it (and assured me that when there is no clear path, it's okay to trample the grass to get where you need to go). While I cannot invite every m-spec person into the physical space, I hope the visitors at Bipanlibrary.com come away feeling a little less poor for resources, and perhaps motivated to find – or create! – similarly reflective spaces on the shelves of their own libraries, schools and homes.

I am so proud of the community I belong to and the history we have made together. Every day I look at my shelves and think, "Here we are. We are so beautiful. What will we do next?"

References

Beauchemin, F. (2016). *How Queer! Personal Narratives from Bisexual, Pansexual, Polysexual, Sexually-Fluid, and Other Non-Monosexual Perspectives*. Atlanta, GA: On Our Own Authority! Publishing.

Chambers, B. (2019). *To Be Taught, If Fortunate*. New York, NY: Harper Voyager.

Fredriksen-Goldsen, K.I.F, Kim, H-J. & Barkan, S.E. (2012). Disability among lesbian, gay, and bisexual adults: Disparities in prevalence and risk. *American Journal of Public Health*, 102(1), e16–e21.

Gailey, S. (2020). *Upright Women Wanted*. New York, NY: Tor Books.

Gary, A. (2017). *The Great Green Room: The Brilliant and Bold Life of Margaret Wise Brown*. New York, NY: Flatiron Books.

Global Philanthropy Project. (2020). *2017–2018 Global ResourcesReport: Government & Philanthropic Support for LGBTI Communities*. https://globalresourcesreport.org/wp-content/uploads/2020/05/GRR_2017-2018_Color.pdf.

Hall, A. (2019). *The Affair of the Mysterious Letter*. New York, NY: Ace Books.

Hemmings, C. (2002). *Bisexual Spaces: A Geography of Sexuality and Gender*. London: Routledge.

Jordan, J. (2002). "Requiem for the Champ" in *Some of Us Did Not Die: New and Selected Essays of June Jordan* (pp.120-124). Washington: Basic Books. (Originally published in *The Progressive*, February 1992)

Kann, C. (2019). *Let's Talk about Love*. New York, NY: Swoon Reads.

Lavery, D. (published under Ortberg, D.M.) (2020). *Something That May Shock and Discredit You*. New York, NY: Atria Books.

Machado, C.M. (2019). *In the Dream House*. Minneapolis, MN: Graywolf Press.

Morgaine, K. (2019). *Pansexuality: A Panoply of Co-Constructed Narratives*. Solana Beach, CA: Cognella Academic Publishing.

Movement Advancement Project (2014) *Understanding Issues Facing Bisexual Americans*. www.lgbtmap.org/file/understanding-issues-facing-bisexual-americans.pdf.

Movement Advancement Project (2016). *Invisible Majority: The Disparities Facing Bisexual People and How to Remedy Them*. www.lgbtmap.org/policy-and-issue-analysis/invisible-majority.

Ochs, R. (1995). *The Bisexual Resource Guide*. Boston, MA: Bisexual Resources Center.

Ochs, R. & Rowley, S.E. (2005). *Getting Bi: Voices of Bisexuals around the World*. Boston, MA: Bisexual Resource Center.

Ochs, R. & Williams, H.S. (2014). *Rec.og.nize: The Voices of Bisexual Men*. Boston, MA: Bisexual Resource Center.

Orndorff, K. (1999). *Bi Lives: Bisexual Women Tell Their Stories*. Tucson, AZ: See Sharp Press.

Philosophy Tube (2022). "Vaccines & Freedom." YouTube. www.youtube.com/watch?v=VaoRCgbywGc.

Piepzna-Samarasinha, L.L. (2018). *Care Work: Dreaming Disability Justice*. Vancouver, Canada: Arsenal Pulp Press.

Rust, P.C. (1995). *Bisexuality and the Challenge to Lesbian Politics*. New York, NY: New York University Press.

Sharpe, T. (2014). *Far from You*. New York, NY: Hyperion.

Storr, M. (1999). *Bisexuality: A Critical Reader*. London: Routledge.

The Bi-bliography. www.librarything.com/catalog/The_Bi-bliography.

The Bisexual Manifesto. *Anything That Moves*, Issue 3 (Summer Winter, 1991). San Francisco, CA: Bay Area Bisexual Network.

Tucker, N.S. (ed.) (1996). *Bisexual Politics: Theories, Queries, and Visions*. London, New York, NY: Harrington Park.

West, Xan (Alexander, Corey) (2016). 'Bisexuality and Me: One Trans Experience'. [Online]. Accessed 03/15/2022 at https://xanwest.wordpress.com/2016/07/20/bisexuality-and-me-one-trans-experience/?preview=true

Yuknavitch, L. (2011). *The Chronology of Water*. Portland, OR: Hawthorne Books.

Additional influential works

Barker, M.J. & Iantaffi, A. (2019). *Life Isn't Binary: On Being Both, Beyond, and In-Between*. London: Jessica Kingsley Publishers.

Bergman, C. & Montgomery, N. (2017). *Joyful Militancy: Building Thriving Resistance in Toxic Times*. Oakland, CA: AK Press.

Brown, A.M. (2017). *Emergent Strategy: Shaping Change, Changing Worlds*. Oakland, CA: AK Press.

Reeve, M. (2017). "Jigsaw: On Bisexual Representation in LGBT+ History." In L. Nickodemus & E. Desmond (eds), *The Bi-ble: Personal Narratives and Essays about Bisexuality*, 127-135. Edinburgh: Monstrous Regiment.

Rose, S. & Stevens, C. (1999). *Bisexual Horizons: Politics, Histories, Lives*. London: Lawrence & Wishart.

Online resources

The Bi-bliography: www.librarything.com/catalog/The_Bibliography
An impressive digital catalog of over 1,600 bisexual and m-spec books, run by Kerri Price between 2015-2019.

The Bi Writer's Association: https://web.archive.org/web/20230324184649/https://www.biwriters.org/
Events and other resources for bisexual writers (and readers!), including the Bisexual Book Awards.

Bi's of Colour: https://bisofcolour.home.blog
From 2010-2021, Bi's of Colour offered community and resources for bisexual people of colour. The blog remains a valuable resource and document of the project's history.

Posi-Pan: Safe haven for pan folks: https://posi-pan.tumblr.com
An impressive compendium of pansexual culture, spanning a century of pansexual representation in literature and other media. The timeline of the term "pansexual" is an essential read.

The Bi History project: https://bihistory.wordpress.com
A physical and digital archive of global bisexual history, run by archivist Mel Reeve. One of very few physical bisexual-focused archives in the world.